Anger, Mercy and the Heart of God

Alex Buchanan

Sovereign World

Sovereign World Ltd
PO Box 777
Tonbridge
Kent TN11 0ZS

ISBN: 1 85240 271 7

This Sovereign World book is distributed in North America by Renew
Books, a ministry of Gospel Light, Ventura, California, USA. For a free
catalog of resources from Renew Books/Gospel Light, please contact your
Christian supplier or call 1-800-4-GOSPEL.

Typeset by CRB Associates, Reepham, Norfolk
Printed in England by Clays Ltd, St Ives plc

Contents

Preface

God gets angry at the devil, who instigated sin in the first place and equally angry with ungodly people and nations. But He also gets angry at His own church when it is sinful and impure.

All mankind are guilty, but perhaps the sinning church is the most guilty because it has access to all the power of God and all His truths in the Bible, which are there to help free them from those things which arouse God's anger.

His anger is certainly aroused by the sinful United Kingdom. We are reaping the consequences of our sinful actions, and seeing the increasing results of God's anger and judgement upon us.

I have said for a long time that I believe we in the UK have only a few more years of liberty left as Christians. Persecution will come largely by legislation and we are already hemmed in by it. We are governed from abroad in many ways. Foreign firms own much of our industry. Indeed, as the Scriptures say, 'How are the mighty fallen.' We were once a mighty nation, but not now.

These things are serious, but we need not be miserable about them because God is with us and He is in control.

God is blessing His church, and He will do so even more in the future. I am believing for revival in our land, but we cannot have revival without persecution and trouble. In the light of this I spend much of my time urging churches and their leaders to toughen up themselves, and their people, so that we will, as the Scripture says, 'Stand in the evil day.' This to me is realism.

When trouble and judgement really strike in greater severity, I expect a large number of church members to turn away from God. Their love will grow cold just as Jesus said, and this will cause them to forsake God and to betray those who remain faithful to God. This has happened right through history in many lands so why should the UK be immune?

The Bible declares that the love of many shall run cold, and in many churches the love of the people is not very hot anyway.

Much now depends on the quality of church leaders. Will they instil the basics of 'The Faith' in us? Will they be strong enough to lead us in these troubled times? I very much hope so. Time will tell!

I believe that God is saying something special to us in the UK and this is what I feel He says:

'I pause to give you a chance to join Me, or to catch up with Me, so that you can work with Me in extending My Kingdom. I am destroying strongholds and I want you to join Me in this great work. I want you to capture the enthusiasm of Heaven; I want you to totally surrender your life to Me. I exhort you, don't lose your place in the front ranks of the overcomers. Join up with Me and change your nation in My power.

'I am looking for those who are willing to become qualified, to lead My church during the difficult and dangerous days which are coming to your nation. These are days in which you will need to share one another's bread, days in which some of you will lay down your lives for My sake.

'I am looking for leaders who will lead My church into vigorous evangelism, into strong warfare and in this warfare sacrifice is inevitable. Such leaders must first prove their love for Me by obedience to My laws, embedding them in their hearts, their homes and in the congregations that they serve. These leaders must have a servant heart, and be free from treachery and empire building. The lust for power and position must be put to death. These leaders must learn to work in close unity, guarding and serving one another and not competing with each other. They must be able to discipline My people without tyranny and to serve them without pride.

'If any are willing to become qualified as leaders, let them now make a decision to do so, and I will respond by giving all the power and the grace necessary for you to be qualified. Join up with Me, let us get on while it is called "Today".'

If we are going to be tough enough to stand in the evil days, we must learn again the basics of our faith. There is no more time for mere Christian entertainment and the preaching of novelties; we must preach stark reality.

There are two basic doctrines missing from much of today's preaching. Things that are basic, essential and healthy. They are **the fear of God**, and **the anger of God**.

Although the main subject of this book is **the anger of God**, the two doctrines are integral. The anger of God should cause us to fear God. The fear of God could enable us escape the anger of God.

There is no fear of God in this world. The Bible declares this awful fact:

> *'There is no fear of God before their eyes.'* (Romans 3:18)

In the world some people may be worshippers of heathen gods and therefore be terrified of them with their ceaseless anger and demands for sacrifice, but this is unhealthy fear, not the fear I am writing about. I am writing about the healthy reverential fear of God.

Many others have no fear of God because they are either unaware of His anger or they prefer to think only of His love. People fear many things – war, sickness, financial need, murder and so on, but Jesus said these words:

> *'And do not fear those who kill the body but cannot kill the soul. But rather fear Him who is able to destroy both soul and body in hell.'* (Matthew 10:28)

God is the one referred to in this scripture, He is the one to fear, and His anger is the thing to beware of.

Leaders bear awful responsibility, because they are given great privileges as the Bible says:

> '... for everyone to whom much is given, from him much will
> be required; and to whom much has been committed, of him
> they will ask the more.' (Luke 12:48)

Church leaders are responsible to teach us the fear of God. Government leaders are responsible to govern in the fear of God, and to make laws that do not rouse God's anger.

Sadly, apart from the Christians in Parliament (for whom I heartily thank God), there are few in our government who have a healthy fear of God and His anger. This government pays no regard to the fact that many of the laws bring God's wrath and judgement upon us. No wonder our nation is in turmoil!

There is not sufficient fear of God in the church either. The anger of God is not a popular subject in preaching today. In fact, few preachers mention it at all in their sermons. And yet, it is vital to the preaching of the whole Gospel. Sermons about the love and grace of God that omit the anger of God may be wonderful, but they are unbalanced. Such sermons might bring many converts, but they will not necessarily produce disciples. We could so very easily portray a caricature of God, as one who is only intent on our blessing rather than on one who is determined to make us like His son, Jesus. This process of conforming us to His image requires God to be angry sometimes, as any good parent would be.

However, I could not write about the anger of God in this book without referring briefly to God's other emotions. We need to consider them in order to deal with His anger in a balanced fashion, seeing that God is not always angry.

I have written about God's **deity** as well as His **humanity**, because we need to understand who God is in order for us not to focus too much on just one aspect of His Being.

Nor can I write dispassionately about the anger of God. I feel an urge to include an appeal to those who read the book who are not yet Christians, in the hope that they may run to God in repentance and so escape His anger. I also hope that Christians who read it and yet harbour sin in their lives, will repent of grieving God and turn to a new life of holiness.

I want this book to draw the attention of God's people to the fear and anger of God in the hope that these essential and healthy doctrines will help us to toughen up for evil days, and be the overcomers that God always wants us to be.

The subject of God's anger is too awful to be read quickly or taken lightly. I hope that readers will not just skim quickly through this book, but will read it thoughtfully.

The chapter on the Cross is relevant because it was there that God showed His anger to the greatest degree.

Alex Buchanan
Burnham
1999

Chapter 1

Various Views of God

Sentimental Views

Some people have the idea that God is always loving and never angry. They reckon that He is a God who smiles on us constantly whatever our behaviour is like. A God who is a kind of glorious first aid box, instantly responsive to our every hurt and need. A God who comes running whenever He hears us cry out to Him, even if we are, at the same time, disobedient to His word.

He is indeed a responsive God, but He does not respond to those who disobey Him. He is loving – after all He loves the whole world:

> *'For God so loved the world that He gave His only begotten Son, that whoever believes in Him should not perish but have everlasting life.'*   (John 3:16)

But God is not sentimental. He does smile on us when our behaviour enables Him to do so, but He can also be angry when it does not please Him.

Mystical Views

The more mystical people regard God as a far-off being, away above the clouds somewhere. A God who only responds to very holy people such as monks, nuns or hermits. To such people God seems to wear a halo, while He looks at the world with a faraway gaze, as though man was incidental to Him.

These mystical types revel in icons, holy relics, wonderful ecclesiastical buildings and monuments. God, to them, is totally unlike man and is, therefore, indescribable and unreachable. They regard a relationship with such a God as virtually impossible.

God is indeed indescribable because there are no words capable of describing Him, and He is unreachable, certainly to the rebellious, because He has decided not to respond to people who are not prepared to follow His ways.

But to those who surrender their lives to Him, He is very approachable and, furthermore, He will reveal Himself to them as far as man can receive such revelation.

Atheistic Views

Atheists say that science proves that we evolved out of primeval slime, and because of this there is no need for a Creator. Such people are generally humanists whose view is that man can be ethical, decent and worthy and they can find self-fulfilment and satisfaction without recourse to a supernatural Being. They regard themselves as their own 'god'. In other words, man does not need God in order to find fulfilment in life. And, after death, we are extinct anyway! So why bother about it? So they say.

They do not agree with the poet who said:

> 'There is a divinity that shapes our ends, rough hew them how we will.'   (Shakespeare)

And yet some of the most famous atheists such as Tom Payne and Voltaire, cried out for God when they were dying. In his more lucid moments before his death, Voltaire said:

> 'If God did not exist it would be necessary to invent Him.'

But Voltaire did not try to find God and it was too late for him, therefore, to enter into the realm in which God had really wanted him to be, which was Heaven.

Many atheists change their views on their deathbed, but unless they cry out for mercy and exercise faith in Jesus, they are doomed.

Agnostic Views

Agnostics say that there may be a God but even if God exists, He is so remote we can never get to Him. Some of these people wish they could get near to God but are not prepared to try too hard because of the demands God might make on them – if He exists. Others, like the mystics previously referred to, say that the possibility of knowing God is so remote that it is not even worth trying to find Him.

Grotesque Views

Such people believe that God loves punishing people. For them He is a God who delights in seeing people burning in the flames of hell, and He resembles the sadistic heathen gods who delight in terrifying people. They see God as a God who loves a good earthquake or some other tragedy. His eyes look all over the world, trying to see what else He can do that would be nasty and cruel. They reckon He is a vengeful God who demands blood every time He is offended. One who punishes us for the least offence against His impossibly high standards. A God who must be constantly appeased by something or other. In fact, the truth is that the Christian faith is the only faith that offers forgiveness and freedom from constant appeasement and fear, so very, very unlike the gods in the minds of those who have a grotesque view of God.

The View that God is Bribeable

Yet other people regard God as someone who is deeply impressed by the fact that they pay their bills and are kind to animals. To such people God can be bribed by their so-called 'righteousness', so that He will not be nasty to them on Judgement Day because He will remember all the good things they have done. Such people forget to read the Bible which says:

> *'But we are all like an unclean thing,*
> *And all our righteousnesses are like filthy rags;*

We all fade as a leaf,
And our iniquities, like the wind,
Have taken us away.'   (Isaiah 64:6)

These people think that God will be aware of all the good works they have done and, therefore, He will praise them when they get to Heaven. They believe they are bound to get there, even if they have not troubled to keep His commandments, or to receive His Son, Jesus, as their Saviour and Lord. But, again, the Bible disagrees, pointing out that salvation is:

'. . . not of works, lest anyone should boast.'

(Ephesians 2:9)

It is a serious thought that those who trust in their good works are actually co-operating with the devil. The devil doesn't mind us doing good works as long as we regard them as a way of salvation, turning us away from the truth that it is Jesus alone who can save us.

None of the views enumerated in this chapter are correct according to the Bible. And, seeing that the Bible is without error, it is best to look into the Scriptures for a correct view of God.

This correct view of God starts in the next chapter.

Chapter 2

The Bible View of God is the Right One

The Bible is the only book that accurately describes God. It gives a balanced, not an unbalanced view of Him. Some people say that the Old Testament view of God is different from the view in the New Testament, but the Old does not contradict the New. In both Testaments God is revealed as loving, caring, tender, but not sentimental, and in both Testaments God is seen to mete out judgement when it is merited.

One of the dangers in writing about one aspect of God, such as His anger, is the danger of imbalance. We could dwell so much on His anger that we forget His love. It is for this reason that I write about other aspects of God, such as His deity, and what He did at Calvary. In that way the reader will not be left feeling scared and hopeless when I focus on the unfashionable aspect of His anger.

My own views expressed in this volume all come from the Bible. For this reason I quote a lot of scriptures, especially in this chapter. It is important for these verses to be meditated on so that they become instilled in our hearts.

God's Deity

Deity means God's uniqueness, His total power, total purity, and His total supremacy. It means that He is over everything in the entire Creation. The Bible is dogmatic when referring to God. God is dogmatic in what He says about Himself. He

can be dogmatic – after all He knows the truth about everything – He is never wrong.

There is no one like God

The Bible says so:

> '...*understand that I am He.*
> *Before Me there was no God formed,*
> *Nor shall there be after Me.*' (Isaiah 43:10)

Find a world ruler who resembles God. Find a holy, saintly, sacrificial person who resembles God. Find the cleverest person in the whole world and see if they are like Him. All such people, if we could find them, would pale into insignificance beside God; there is just no comparison. Truly, there is no one like God.

Therefore there is no other god to challenge Him

No one will replace God, He is utterly unique. Again the Bible declares this:

> '*Thus says the* LORD, *the King of Israel,*
> *And His Redeemer, the* LORD *of hosts:*
> "*I* **am** *the First and I* **am** *the Last;*
> *Besides Me* **there is** *no God.*"' (Isaiah 44:6)

Some people are bound to be enraged by such a dogmatic statement, their hackles will rise when they read it, but God is only telling the truth about Himself. He does not lie. Who is there who can contradict Him?

He is the Creator

This inimitable God created everything. This world and this universe did not evolve. Scripture declares the truth:

> '...*the everlasting God, the* LORD,
> *The Creator of the ends of the earth,*
> *Neither faints nor is weary.*
> *There is no searching of His understanding.*' (Isaiah 40:28)

Nothing was created by any other being or by any other method (Colossians 1:16).

It is God who created the billions and billions of stars,

planets, polestars and other amazing things that scientists are discovering today. This is in addition to all the wonderful things in the micro world such as the atom and small creatures. When we take a drop of water and put it under a microscope it teems with little beings of one sort or another, and God created them all.

There are 32,000,000 species of insects and some of them are very, very small. Yet God created them and keeps His eyes on them. It is so foolish to believe that these things just appeared as the evolutionists insist.

Evolution is not an alternative to creation. It is not even a theory. It is only a hypothesis without any evidence to support it. Evolutionists try to rake up evidence, like missing links and so on, but they fail miserably every single time. There is not a shred of evidence to prove, let alone point to, evolution.

The more scientists explore this universe, the more evidence is uncovered proving the Bible to be right when it says that God created everything. No human mind could even have conceived the plan of creation, and no human would have had the power to bring it into being anyway. Nor could any human control and sustain it. But the God of the Bible conceived the plan of Creation in His mind. He had the power to bring it into being – and He did, and He has the power to control and sustain it – and He does.

God is the God of the Nations

'For the kingdom is the LORD's,
And He rules over the nations.'　　　　　(Psalm 22:28)

'God reigns over the nations;
God sits on His holy throne.'　　　　　(Psalm 47:8)

Many world leaders think that they rule their nation by their own abilities. When we look on our TV screens and see these strutting leaders pontificating, speaking about their great exploits, and how they govern their nation and lead their land, they really do look quite ridiculous.

Now some of them do have a measure of success in leading their nation, but where is the leader who can adequately govern his own land, let alone the nations of the world? Where is a leader who can bring the entire world's nations together and cause them to issue a cohesive bulletin after their summit conferences?

There is only one answer to the question 'who can control the nations?' The answer is – only God. This world's rulers forget that power to rule is given only by God, and this can be removed from them by Him at any time. He does raise them up and give them a measure of ability, but when pride creeps in God brings them down.

God is all powerful

'Ah, Lord GOD! Behold, You have made the heavens and the earth by Your great power and outstretched arm. There is nothing too hard for You.'   (Jeremiah 32:17)

Men and women are clever. They are powerful, they carry out tremendous exploits. They send rockets to the moon; they produce new drugs, which help human beings. Civil engineers build huge dams, tunnels, railways and motorways. People are very, very clever. But none of them are all powerful, they are all fallible, they have weaknesses and, in any case, after many years, their powers diminish, they get older, their brains decay and they die. But God never dies. He is all powerful, He remains powerful because His powers never diminish.

God is all seeing

*'For the eyes of the LORD run to and fro throughout the whole earth, to show Himself strong on behalf of **those** whose heart is loyal to Him. In this you have done foolishly; therefore from now on you shall have wars.'*   (2 Chronicles 16:9)

*'And there is no creature hidden from His sight, but all things are naked and open to the eyes of Him to whom we **must** give account.'*   (Hebrews 4:13)

God does not miss one ant scurrying across a forest floor. He keeps track of the hairs on the heads of six billion people.

He doesn't miss one thought going through each of their minds. Truly God does not miss a thing.

God's Humanity

All that I have written about God could make Him seem rather remote, or even unfeeling, so let me now enlarge on His humanity. Having written about His deity, His power, His supremacy, now let me write about His humanity and show that He is very far from being unfeeling or remote. I am using verses from the Old Testament in this section.

He is a forgiving God

This wonderful verse proves it:

> *'Let the wicked forsake his way,*
> *And the unrighteous man his thoughts;*
> *Let him return to the* LORD,
> *And He will have mercy on him;*
> *And to our God,*
> *For He will abundantly pardon.'*   (Isaiah 55:7)

Name the world's worst sinner. Whoever he or she might be – the greatest murderer, the perpetrator of the greatest genocide, the most evil person you can think of – and I will say that however terrible his or her crimes have been, God will forgive them as long as they bow before Him and become truly repentant.

Some of the Nazi leaders from the last war were in prison at Nuremberg, being judged for their crimes. An American padre went to witness to them about Jesus and several of those wicked, wicked, evil men repented, turned to Jesus Christ, received His salvation and became born again Christians. There are plenty of testimonies to back this up. It proves the point that however evil men and women are or however low they sink, if there is true repentance there can be regeneration for them and they can be born again.

This underlines God's humanity. He will forgive anyone if they repent.

He is a compassionate God

Far more so than any human father:

> 'As a father pities his children,
> So the LORD pities those who fear Him.
> For He knows our frame;
> He remembers that we are dust.' (Psalm 103:13–14)

This verse refers to the tremendous compassion of God who is so great and yet no earthly father can feel more compassion. Wasn't it Jesus' compassion that kept Him spreadeagled on the Cross looking at those He came to save, spitting at Him and rejecting Him? Amazingly He still remained compassionate. What a God – what a Saviour!

He is a caring God

> 'Can a woman forget her nursing child,
> And not have compassion on the son of her womb?
> Surely they may forget,
> Yet I will not forget you.' (Isaiah 49:15)

So God is not just an impassive Creator who is only mildly interested in the world He created and those He caused to live in it, but He is a God who is loving, warm hearted, generous, and caring. He is very interested in mankind and He cares for every living creature, all six billion people who are presently on the earth, He cares for every individual. Sometimes appearances would seem to deny that when we look at all the suffering in the world. But that does not alter the character of God, He is caring. And, of course, as we survey the misery in the world, we must not overlook all the good in the world, all the wonderful things that God is doing through His Church and the many great relief agencies.

Having said this, the Bible also declares that He is not sentimental. He will chastise His people, but only for their good, and to show the truth that He cares for us.

This God is wholly righteous, demanding righteousness from His born again people, but He is also a God who has made a way for us through Jesus to be made righteous in His sight. Scripture says that mankind's destiny is to know God, to be like God, to steward the world with God, both on this earth and on the new earth, and to be with Him in Heaven. Surely the fact that God offers such a destiny to all those who want to take advantage of it, shows that He is forgiving, compassionate and caring.

So the Bible Reveals a Mighty Holy God, but One Who Has Feelings

God created man in His own image:

> *'Then God said, "Let Us make man in Our image, according to Our likeness;..."'* (Genesis 1:26)

God has feelings, therefore we humans, made in His image, have feelings like His. Feelings such as love, grief, joy and anger. God has created us to be like Him in every thing except His deity, and that belongs to Him alone.

God's feelings are always in balance

One of the mysterious things about God is that He can be loving and angry in equal strength, at the same time. When He is angry He is still loving, when He is loving He can still be angry, and the Bible shows this:

> *'Moses took his tent and pitched it outside the camp, far from the camp, and called it the tabernacle of meeting. And it came to pass that everyone who sought the LORD went out to the tabernacle of meeting which was outside the camp.'*
> (Exodus 33:7)

God's anger does not alter His love. He never gets so angry that He forgets to be loving, but nor does He become so loving that He overlooks the sin that makes Him angry.

> *'You answered them, O LORD our God;*
> *You were to them God-Who-Forgives,*
> *Though You took vengeance on their deeds.'* (Psalm 99:8)

God loves us enough to forgive us, but He is angry enough to punish us when it is necessary. His anger is always tempered with mercy; the Scripture is shot through with illustrations of this. There is always an escape from His anger and judgement, but it is only by repentance and faith. The moment God sees these things in us, He stops being angry, manifests His love, and gives us His grace.

We, as human beings, are not like God in the fact that our emotions are not perfectly balanced. If we get angry with our children, we still love them, but sometimes our anger is stronger than our love. But God's anger is an integral part of His love; the one emotion of His balances the other. In fact, love, without the element of anger, is pure sentimentality.

Some human fathers are guilty of great imbalance. They are either too strict with their children, perhaps continually moving the goalposts, never satisfied with their children's achievements and behaviour, never giving them encouragement. Such fathers never give their children the healthy cuddles that they have needed. So, they are unbalanced fathers, and their emotions are unbalanced.

Other fathers are too lax. They never check their children's behaviour at all, however bad it becomes. Now the father who says that he is a loving father yet is lax in his treatment of his children when they misbehave, is merely sentimental. He is not really loving at all.

A loving father has to be angry sometimes, when bad behaviour merits it. By the way, it is possible as parents to be angry without sinning. The Bible says that this is possible:

> *'Be angry, and do not sin: do not let the sun go down on your wrath.'*   (Ephesians 4:26)

Of course, having said all these things, some fathers are simply not interested in their children's lives at all. This is the ultimate tragedy for children. It is so sad that very many children grow up with a distorted view of God because of their distorted role model in their fathers. God grant that fathers might become balanced in their emotions like God, loving, angry, caring and so on. May God help us to be like this if we are parents.

Chapter 3

God Is Seen in Jesus

All that I wrote in the previous chapter about God is true of Jesus. I used Old Testament verses in the previous chapter, now I am using verses from the New Testament, which is all about Jesus who is God the Son.

I do not understand how the Father, the Son and the Holy Spirit can be three in one, separate and yet one. An often used illustration is that of water, ice, and steam. All are water, but in different forms. This can be helpful, but it is not perfect. I have given up trying to work it out. In any case, the human mind is too small to do so, so I am prepared to simply believe this now and find out the complete answer when I get to Heaven.

Jesus is God and man. I don't understand how He can be both at once, but then who can? Greater minds than mine have wrestled with this truth and not understood it, so I believe it is better to believe the Scriptures than to engage in endless conjecture and therefore waste the opportunity to enter our destiny. Our destiny is, of course, to know God through Jesus.

Jesus Is God

Some heresies try to alter the Bible to deny the divinity of Jesus, but it plainly declares the fact of it:

> *'In the beginning was the Word, and the Word was with God, and the Word was God. He was in the beginning with God.'*
>
> (John 1:1–2)

A word is the expression of the one who utters it. Jesus expressed God in a form which was bearable to mankind.

Most other religions deny the truth of this statement, but I believe the Bible and in it Jesus declares categorically that He is God:

> *'I and My Father are one.'* (John 10:30)

He was in the beginning with God. He is not inferior to the Father, or to God the Holy Spirit. They are all equal and they are so united in their essence that one person of the Godhead will never work against the others.

Jesus expressed God's deity and His humanity. His humanity gives us hope. Far from being an impassive God, He came and lived among us, pulsating with love and life. Jesus shows us an outreaching God, with arms spread wide, even to the sinful and unlovely, such as a disfigured leper and a treacherous Judas.

Everything that God wanted us to know and understand was communicated in, through and by the Lord Jesus.

> *'And the Word became flesh and dwelt among us, and we beheld His glory, the glory as of the only begotten of the Father, full of grace and truth.'* (John 1:14)

His Deity

Jesus is divine, just as the Father and the Spirit are divine. Jesus Himself testified to the truth of this in the scripture when they came to arrest Him in Gethsemane. He used the Divine Name:

> *'They answered Him, "Jesus of Nazareth." Jesus said to them, "I am **He**." And Judas, who betrayed Him, also stood with them. Now when He said to them, "I am **He**," they drew back and fell to the ground.'* (John 18:5–6)

Jesus is the Creator

The Old Testament declares that God is the Creator – the New Testament declares that Jesus is the Creator. There is no contradiction because Jesus is God.

> *'For by Him all things were created that are in heaven and that are on earth, visible and invisible, whether thrones or dominions or principalities or powers. All things were created through Him and for Him. And He is before all things, and in Him all things consist.'* (Colossians 1:16–17)

Jesus is the upholder of Heaven and earth

Hebrews describes Him so wonderfully:

> *'who being the brightness of His glory and the express image of His person, and upholding all things by the word of His power, when He had by Himself purged our sins, sat down at the right hand of the Majesty on high.'* (Hebrews 1:3)

By the way, have you ever imagined the chaos there would have been in the universe if, at Calvary, the one who upholds the whole universe had failed? If one irritable thought had been allowed to enter His mind at Calvary the plan of salvation would have failed because Jesus would have failed, and if He was upholding the universe, and He failed, what would have happened to it?

Jesus is the God of all nations

In the Day of Judgement every one in Creation will see that the nations only had one real Head.

> *'Who shall not fear You, O Lord, and glorify Your name? For You alone are holy. For all nations shall come and worship before You, For Your judgments have been manifested.'*
>
> (Revelation 15:4)

Jesus is all powerful

In that Day His power will be displayed in its entirety.

> *'And Jesus came and spoke to them, saying, "All authority has been given to Me in heaven and on earth." '*
>
> (Matthew 28:18)

Jesus is all knowing and all seeing

As I described the omniscience of God from the Old Testament – I am now showing it from the New Testament:

> *'...And He said to Him, "Lord, You know all things...."'*
> (John 21:17)

> *'And there is no creature hidden from His sight, but all things are naked and open to the eyes of Him to whom we must give account.'*   (Hebrews 4:13)

His Humanity

The humanity of God the Father and that of God the Holy Spirit was seen in Jesus. He gave us a bearable manifestation of God's glory. If God had appeared in all His glory everybody would have died on the spot. Jesus came to show it in human form so that we could bear that manifestation. Now Jesus was a real man, He was not God camouflaged by a human body. He didn't wear a halo. He lived in a miserable body, He toiled in a real job, He ate, He slept, He walked around, He saw, He heard and He thought just as we do. He showed that God has feelings. Let me enlarge on this.

Jesus got tired

He was a real man with the same needs that we have. The life He led, with its demands of teaching, preaching, healing and delivering obviously made Him tired.

> *'Now Jacob's well was there. Jesus therefore, being wearied from His journey, sat thus by the well. It was about the sixth hour.'*   (John 4:6)

Jesus got hungry and thirsty

He could not do without food or water any more than we can. Try fasting for nearly six weeks and see if you feel hungry!

> *'And when He had fasted forty days and forty nights, afterward He was hungry.'*   (Matthew 4:2)

Jesus was tempted

One of the most staggering things about Jesus is that He went through all the temptations we go through! When I think of my temptations I can scarcely believe that He went through them too. But He did – and He overcame them all!

> *'For we do not have a High Priest who cannot sympathize with our weaknesses, but was in all points tempted as we are, yet without sin.'* (Hebrews 4:15)

Imagine being dogged every moment by the devil himself, day and night for six weeks. This most cunning being brought every temptation he could against Jesus' body, mind, and spirit!

> *'being tempted for forty days by the devil.'* (Luke 4:2)

But the devil failed to bring Jesus down.

Jesus suffered

He suffered pain, both physical, emotional and mental. He suffered rejection, He suffered tremendous misunderstanding. That is why He can sympathise with us – and why He can enable us to overcome as He did.

> *'For we do not have a High Priest who cannot sympathize with our weaknesses, but was in all points tempted as we are, yet without sin.'* (Hebrews 4:15)

> *'Though He was a Son, yet He learned obedience by the things which He suffered.'* (Hebrews 5:8)

God's Feelings Are Seen in Jesus

Jesus is a God who feels love (as Scripture says in John 3:16), and the full range of emotions.

He feels anger

> *'And when He had looked around at them with anger, being grieved by the hardness of their hearts, He said to the man, "Stretch out your hand." And He stretched it out, and His hand was restored as whole as the other.'* (Mark 3:5)

Contrary to what some theologians say, the anger of God is not only seen in the Old Testament, for they say that it shows a God of wrath while the New Testament shows a God of grace. But, in fact, the anger and the grace of God are seen in both the Old Testament and the New Testament. They do not contradict each other. The New Testament speaks about the anger of God:

> *'and said to the mountains and rocks, "Fall on us and hide us from the face of Him who sits on the throne and from the wrath of the Lamb! For the great day of His wrath has come, and who is able to stand?"'*   (Revelation 6:16–17)

He feels grief

In the same verse that describes His anger, we see His grief too:

> *'And when He had looked around at them with anger, being grieved by the hardness of their hearts, He said to the man, "Stretch out your hand." And he stretched it out, and his hand was restored as whole as the other.'*   (Mark 3:5)

He feels joy

God is never miserable, even when He is angry:

> *'In that hour Jesus rejoiced in the Spirit and said, "I thank You, Father, Lord of heaven and earth, that You have hidden these things from the wise and prudent and revealed them to babes. Even so, Father, for so it seemed good in Your sight."'*
> (Luke 10:21)

Jesus is so full of joy that He wants to share it with all who love Him:

> *'These things I have spoken to you, that My joy may remain in you, and that your joy may be full.'*   (John 15:11)

He feels compassion

When Jesus looks at those who are in need of His help, He responds to them wholeheartedly and reaches out to supply their needs:

> *'So Jesus had compassion and touched their eyes. And immediately their eyes received sight, and they followed Him.'*
> (Matthew 20:34)

He Loves Righteousness and Hates Iniquity

God does not like righteousness – He loves it! He does not merely dislike sin – He hates it with a holy hatred:

> *'You have loved righteousness and hated lawlessness;*
> *Therefore God, Your God, has anointed You*
> *With the oil of gladness more than Your companions.'*
>
> (Hebrews1:9)

All Christians should be the same.

So then, the Bible declares a God who is Holy, a supreme Creator, one before whom we must bow down in reverence and submission. But it also shows us a tender hearted, compassionate God, who feels for us in our weaknesses. His feelings are not the mercurial up and down feelings common to us. He is not a sad God who must be cheered up, nor a needy God for whom we must provide. He is not an angry deity who we must appease. His anger does not blow hot and cold, nor does His love wax and wane. His love is a firm love, which never degenerates into mere sentimentality, and His anger is pure and completely free from malice.

For the purposes of this book I will now concentrate on one of God's emotions. Namely His anger.

Chapter 4

God Gets Angry

God is Continuously Angry with Satan

His anger will never be removed from the devil who ruined His world. But His anger is not a vindictive anger, but a just anger. Satan ruined God's world and ruined His whole creation. He ruined the people that God created to love Him. That roused the anger of God so much that it will never be removed from Satan.

Sin makes God angry. Satan is continually sinful and does not, and will not, change, therefore God has to be continually angry with him, and of course, with all those who choose to follow him.

God Gets Angry with the Nations

When the nations of this world follow the devil in preference to following the Son of God, then God gets angry with them and judges them. God has judged the nations right through history when they had deliberately gone the way of evil. God has put them down because of their sin. God raises up nations and empires, and He puts them down. He raises them up when they are righteous and He puts them down when they are sinful. History records this.

God also Gets Angry with His Church

When His Church sins it angers God. Everyone who sins is guilty and bears the anger of God, but perhaps the sinning Church is the most guilty, because it has access to all the power of God, and all the truths in the Bible to help it be free of those things that arouse God's anger.

Some of the major reasons why God gets angry with His Church are:

1. Church splits and squabbles.
2. Tyrannical leaders.
3. Ultra-democratic people.
4. Misuse of God's money.
5. Celebrations and conferences that are merely Christian entertainment.

God Will Not Always Be in a State of Anger

God will not always be in a state of anger, except, of course, in His anger against the devil.

As far as mankind is concerned He is not angry with them all the time. His grace will ensure that this is true. The Bible points this out in fact:

> *'He will not always strive with us,*
> *Nor will He keep His anger forever.'*   (Psalm 103:9)

The expression 'keep His anger', in the Hebrew means 'to cherish anger', or 'to bear a grudge'. God is saying that He is not malicious and that He does not harbour a vengeful spirit.

He will never be angry at all in Heaven because there will never be anything there to arouse His anger.

God dearly loves mankind and He is willing to forgive their sin, but if they reject His love, His anger is aroused and if people continue in their rejection, then His anger remains upon them forever in Hell.

It is important not to think that God is continually looking at the inhabitants in Hell and gloating over their sorrows in fierce anger. That is not true. The fact is that His anger is a condition in which all in Hell exist.

The Fact That God Gets Angry Is an Unpopular Truth

It is offensive to many who say that God is love and therefore He does not get angry, especially with those who have lived good lives, and do good deeds. But I repeat, it is not possible for anyone to gain God's favour by good works. The so-called good works of non-Christians are not acceptable to God at all. Not only does God reject these good works, He is angry with the people because they try to substitute their good works for the requirements of God, namely surrender to Jesus. The Bibles says:

> *'For by grace you have been saved through faith, and that not of yourselves; it is the gift of God, not of works, lest anyone should boast.'* (Ephesians 2:8–9)

Again:

> *'God is a just judge,*
> *And God is angry with the wicked every day.'* (Psalm 7:11)

Primarily God's anger is directed against Satan, but if men choose to align themselves with the devil (and all who deliberately sin do so) then they must bear the weight of God's fierce anger because they side with God's enemy.

Some damage has been done by the more extreme Christians in a previous age. For some, although not all, of the Puritan Christians went too far in their portrayal of God as one who seemed to be permanently angry with mankind. They portrayed a God with glaring eyes, who punished the slightest misdeed with awful punishment. They spoke more about His anger and His demands than they spoke about His love. Many of their descendants, therefore, grew up with a morbid fear of God and their lives were blighted and joyless. Sadly this created a caricature of God in their minds. However, there is no need for us to perpetuate this caricature of God, if we are prepared to search the Bible for a balanced view of Him.

God Is Not Angry Without Reason

God gets angry because of the harm that sin does to His world and His people. And never forget that God is angry about bad things, not good things. He is angry about things that harm us. So, His anger is beneficial. God cares for us and when He sees the ravages of sin in the human body through drug addiction, alcoholism, immorality and sexual perversion, He gets angry both with Satan, who is the prime mover behind all this sin, and with the men and women who desecrate their own bodies or those of others to whom they introduce their sin.

God only gets angry when it is necessary. If He just left the world to get on with its sin and turned away from us, then there would be no restraint at all in the world. Satan would be able to do what he wanted. But, God, in His love and wisdom, got angry and took drastic action against Satan, and those who follow him. So His anger is necessary if this world is not to be totally ruined by sin.

The Bible does not say anywhere that God is anger, but it does say that He is **love**:

> *'He who does not love does not know God, for God is love.'*
> (1 John 4:8)

By the way, when we think of God's anger we must clearly distinguish between human and divine anger. The one is not the same as the other. Human anger usually has malice in it and loss of control. God's anger is not like this. It has no malice at all in it, and it is a controlled anger because it is pure anger.

God Sees All Sin

God is very attentive to this world and all its people. He looks on the billions of people on this earth and not one of them is hidden from Him. Nothing they say, do or think is hidden because God is very, very attentive. He sees sin, therefore, wherever it is committed.

> *'The eyes of the LORD are in every place,*
> *Keeping watch on the evil and the good.'* (Proverbs 15:3)

King David realised that God could see everything and everyone. That is why he said:

> *'Where can I go from Your Spirit?*
> *Or where can I flee from Your presence?'* (Psalm 139:7)

In fact, as I indicated in a previous chapter, there is no hiding place left in the world, humanly speaking. Spy cameras are up in the sky, apparently able to see a car number plate. Cameras are in city centres able to spot the shopping in a basket.

Zoom lens cameras spy on the famous wherever they go. So, where are our hiding places from our fellow men and women? If our modern gadgets can show us so much, how much more can be seen by God who never sleeps, never gets tired and inattentive, and who cannot be fooled by anyone?

Criminals think they get away with their crimes because they are undetected by the police. In some cases they succeed. But, they will never escape the court of Heaven in the great Day of Judgement. All their crimes will be recorded and will be read out before them up there. So, God sees all sin wherever it is committed.

When God Sees Sin He Hates it

When God sees sin it does not leave Him unmoved, and He cannot turn a blind eye to it. If He did, He would not be a righteous God. Sin arouses God's anger and brings the consequent judgement upon those who persist in it. The prophet knew this in the Old Testament times when he said:

> 'You are of purer eyes than to behold evil,
> And cannot look on wickedness. . . . '   (Habakkuk 1:13)

This verse does not say that God cannot see sin, it means that He cannot remain unmoved in the light of it. As I said before, when God sees sin He does not merely dislike it, He hates it.

Anger, therefore, is the only possible attitude that God can have towards sin. How can He do otherwise? He does not fly into a temper but He maintains His repugnance to sin, His judgement against it and His determination to deal with it. His anger is always a just anger for it is based on His perfect assessment of every situation.

If we know of sin in our lives, remember that God sees it clearly, and He is not fooled even if we retain our sin but carry on with church life. It is best to deal with it now, however embarrassing it may be. It is better to confess our sin, forsake it and receive God's whole-hearted forgiveness rather than being embarrassed in the sight and hearing of the whole of Heaven. Think how gracious God is. The woman taken in adultery received God's graciousness in the person of Jesus (John 8:10–11). His attitude is just the same today. Why not believe it and rejoice in it?

Chapter 5

The Causes of God's Anger

There Are Several Major Causes of God's Anger

1. The devil and his activities, together with all humans that follow him.
2. The nations who reject His laws.
3. The Church when it is impure.

But All Sin Makes God Angry

Man's definition of sin takes many forms. Some say that sin is simply weakness in various areas of life, while others think that some sins are worse than others. But, God regards all sin as sin. There are no degrees of sin in His estimation. Another thing to remember is that all sin is against God. We may think that we sin against one another, and there is some truth in that fact. But in the last analysis all sin is against God because God is the one who is offended by it. King David put it well in the Psalms:

> 'Against You, You only, have I sinned,
> And done this evil in Your sight;
> That You may be found just when You speak,
> And blameless when You judge.'   (Psalm 51:4)

The Only Proper Definition of Sin is Found in the Bible

Basically, sin is offence against God. If we break the laws of the land we commit an offence. Similarly, if we break the laws of God, we commit an offence against Him. There are several terms for sin.

Transgression

Transgression means that we go beyond boundaries that have been set. God has set boundaries and we sin if we go beyond them. For example, God has set sexual boundaries, one man to one woman in marriage. Homosexuals go beyond God's boundary and they will suffer for it. In Bible times that penalty was death:

> 'If a man lies with a male as he lies with a woman, both of them have committed an abomination. They shall surely be put to death. Their blood shall be upon them.'
>
> (Leviticus 20:13)

Trespass

Trespass means going into areas to which we are not entitled to go. Glory and worship belong to God alone. If we give glory to ourselves, or give it to anyone else, we trespass on God's territory. When we worship a sports personality, or anyone else, we go into a forbidden area. God has said that we must worship only Him because He alone deserves the worship of mankind.

Rebellion

Rebellion is breaking the laws of God which He has set for all mankind. Not just for some, but for all mankind. The laws of God may seem hard but they are actually very good. God did not make them to be oppressive for us, He made them to be a blessing and a safeguard for us. A fence around a cliff top is not oppressive, it is a lifesaver. If there were not laws and standards in the world, such as God's laws, it would be in total anarchy.

Humanists will say that sin is relative to their own personal standards. In other words, man makes his own laws and he does what he thinks is right. But, if different men make their own laws, how will they know whose law they are transgressing? This is confusion.

The only safeguard is God, and His laws. After all, He is all-wise and men are only partly wise. He is a perfect judge, but the best human judges are fallible. They are not always righteous.

Rebellion Is Sin Against God

Rebellion is the natural state of every new born child coming into this world. It is the original sin implanted in all of us by Satan after he introduced sin into the world in the first place. King David mourned over his inherent sin in scripture:

> *'Behold, I was brought forth in iniquity,*
> *And in sin my mother conceived me.'*   (Psalm 51:5)

Surely every parent believes in original sin. There is no such thing as an innocent child, nor is there such a thing as an innocent nation. Even if people are well behaved, good to others and fairly unselfish, they are still guilty of the greatest crime, which I write about later in the chapter.

A professor was once debating Christianity with his students. A student shouted out saying, 'Surely you do not believe in original sin.' The professor said, 'Of course I do!' The student said, 'Why do you believe such a myth?' The professor said, 'Simple, I have four children.'

The nation of Israel was rebellious against God

Time after time, despite God's goodness to them, the Israelites turned against Him. Moses had to say to them:

> *'Remember do not forget how you provoked the LORD your*
> *God to wrath in the wilderness. From the day that you*
> *departed from the land of Egypt until you came to this place,*
> *you have been rebellious against the LORD.'*
>
> (Deuteronomy 9:7)

Not satisfied with being led by God alone, they demanded a king to lead them, but when they got one he turned out to be as bad as they were. The prophet had to go to King Saul and point out how seriously God regarded sin and rebellion. He said:

> *'For rebellion is as the sin of witchcraft,*
> *And stubbornness is as iniquity and idolatry.*

> *Because you have rejected the word of the* LORD,
> *He also has rejected you from being king.'*
>
> (1 Samuel 15:23)

Therefore Israelite children were rebellious against God

Their parents were rebellious, they inherited a rebellious streak and they were rebellious people. They, in turn, trained their children to be the same. King David prayed about children and asked that they:

> *'... may not be like their fathers,*
> *A stubborn and rebellious generation,*
> *A generation that did not set its heart aright,*
> *And whose spirit was not faithful to God.'*   (Psalm 78:8)

God viewed this rebelliousness as so serious that drastic punishment was prescribed.

> *'If a man has a stubborn and rebellious son who will not obey the voice of his father or the voice of his mother, and who, when they have chastened him, will not heed them, then his father and his mother shall take hold of him and bring him out to the elders of his city, to the gate of his city. And they shall say to the elders of his city, "This son of ours is stubborn and rebellious; he will not obey our voice; he is a glutton and a drunkard."'*   (Deuteronomy 21:18–20)

Just in case we judge the Israelites for their sin, we do well to consider our own behaviour and that of our children. If there were more discipline in the home there would be less crime on the streets. Permissive parents produce rebellious children.

Disobedience Is Sin Against God

> *'Let no one deceive you with empty words, for because of these things the wrath of God comes upon the sons of disobedience.'*   (Ephesians 5:6)

Disobedience is the result of a rebellious spirit and it brings the anger of God upon us. One of the first words a baby learns is not 'yes', but 'no'. Its first impulse is to get its own way. If that doesn't work, then the child will make a nuisance of itself so that its parents will give in to it.

This is the essence of rebellion and disobedience. If the child is not checked it will grow into a perpetual rebel.

It was this knowledge that caused God to wipe out the Amalekites, including women and children. He knew that they would grow up to be cruel, self-willed destroyers of surrounding nations. So was God unjust and unrighteously angry? No, He was merciful to the surrounding nations when He destroyed the Amalekites who would have destroyed them.

In our day, we do well to heed God's word when He speaks to us about disobedience.

Rebellion Is Usually Against Laws or Government

All governments enact laws, if they did not, anarchy would prevail. But there are always people who will either disobey those laws, or who try to remove them. Or, in addition, some try to change them and legalise abhorrent things such as sodomy, i.e. homosexual activity.

The worst thing is that when governments change or nullify God's laws. God gave me this prophecy some time ago:

> 'I am looking over your nation, seeing everything and this is My accusation. The leaders of the nation have moved My landmarks, My laws, therefore My judgement has come to the nation and it will continue to come in greater severity. Remember what I have written: " 'Cursed is the one who moves his neighbor's landmark.' And all the people shall say, 'Amen!' " (Deuteronomy 27:17).
>
> 'And yet I gave My laws to be safeguards and a means of blessing to mankind. Many leaders in My own Church have removed My landmarks, My laws, therefore I am shaking My Church in severe judgement. Let My shepherds also remember what I have written.
>
> 'Calvary shows the depths of My anger against lawlessness. It was there that I removed the curse of the law from My people, but I did not remove their

obligation to honour My law. So, I look now for those who will restore My laws to a place of priority in their hearts, their homes and their congregations. I look for holiness, integrity and obedience in those who bear My name. If I see a response in this way, I may yet use you to save your nation from My total judgement. So I offer you a hope and a way of escape to see if you will obey My word and pray for your nation, and honour My laws. Respond speedily lest My full judgement be poured out upon you. If any would count the cost of obedience to My laws, let them consider Calvary again.'

God likened His laws to the property boundaries, which were transgressed on pain of death in the nation of Israel.

> ' "Cursed is the one who moves his neighbour's landmark."
> And all the people shall say, "Amen!" '
>
> (Deuteronomy 27:17)

> 'The princes of Judah are like those who remove a
>   landmark;
> I will pour out my wrath on them like water.' (Hosea 5:10)

The old prophets had a thankless task when they brought the Word of God to their people. The response was often as illustrated in this verse:

> 'As for the word that you have spoken to us in the name of
> the LORD, we will not listen to you!'   (Jeremiah 44:16)

Disobedience, whether in people or government, arouses God's anger, and brings His inevitable punishment. And yet, obedience to God's laws brings blessings (Psalm 19:11). Why are we so stupid as to refuse His blessings by our disobedience to His laws?

> 'Moreover by them Your servant is warned,
> And in keeping them there is great reward.'   (Psalm 19:11)

But No-one Can Really Remove God's Laws

Men may seem to do so, but when a nation replaces God's laws with its own, it sows the seeds of its own destruction.

The nation may seem to thrive for a while, but because all human laws are flawed and mostly not kept, trouble comes. Human laws are made, ignored, re-drafted and ignored again. They have to be because they are flawed. God's laws are perfect, safe and beneficial. They cannot be destroyed, even though they may not be kept.

> '... the word of God came (and the Scripture cannot be broken).   (John 10:35)

God has ordained His laws for ever:

> 'Forever, O LORD,
> Your word is settled in heaven.'   (Psalm 119:89)

Carelessness Is Sin Against God

Carelessness is sin against God. Carelessness may be unconscious disobedience, but it is still punished by God. Carelessness is the failure to remember who God is, and the rules He has laid down. The lack of godly fear is a reason why God pours out His anger, both on earth and in hell.

In the Old Testament there was a man called Uzzah, a Levite, but he was a careless Levite. He should have known better than to take the sacred Ark and shove it on a cart. So, because of his carelessness he died.

> 'Then the anger of the LORD was aroused against Uzzah, and God struck him there for his error; and he died there by the ark of God.'   (2 Samuel 6:7)

Because he was a Levite, Uzzah knew very well that the Ark should have been carried with poles, not on a cart. David also knew that law, so they were both guilty of the sin of carelessness, and they suffered for it seriously.

Idolatry Is a Sin Against God

There are many modern 'idols' or 'gods'. They can be football stars, pop singers, musicians or racing drivers. There is nothing intrinsically wrong with any of these sports or occupations. God is not against enjoyment, but when these things become all-absorbing then idolatry begins. On the face of it, hero worship seems to be fairly normal. It doesn't seem to do any harm to idolise a pop star, or any other famous person. But if more attention is given to the idols rather than the God who made them, then we are guilty of the worship of mankind. The hysterical scenes in cities where victorious football teams come home is an evidence of such idolatry.

There are other forms of worship too. Some worship money, their property, their work or their homes. The object of our worship does not matter, the fact that we give to these things, or people, the worship and excessive attention which is due only to God makes us guilty in the eyes of God.

God expressed His anger and grief on this idolatry in the Bible:

> *'Because they have forsaken Me and burned incense to other gods, that they might provoke Me to anger with all the works of their hands. Therefore My wrath shall be aroused against this place and shall not be quenched.'*   (2 Kings 22:17)

Some people may argue that we don't burn incense to sportsmen, and of course we don't actually do such a thing. But this 'burning incense' can take place in the heart too. If man worships strange gods, whatever form these gods take in this world, then God will make sure that they worship them, or the demons who inspired them to idolise human beings, forever, in hell! There they will find out that their gods were actually deceiving demons operating through men and women who allowed pride to enter their hearts, thus opening the way for demons to possess them.

Immorality Is Sin Against God

The Bible shows how strongly God hates immorality in whatever form it takes. He hates it so strongly that He says it should not even be mentioned.

> *'But fornication and all uncleanness or covetousness, let it not even be named among you, as is fitting for saints.'*
> (Ephesians 5:3)

God asks us to put immorality to death in our hearts – so it must be possible!

> *'Therefore put to death your members which are on the earth: fornication, uncleanness, passion, evil desire, and covetousness, which is idolatry.'*   (Colossians 3:5)

Another sure sign that a nation is in decay is the rise of homosexual and lesbian behaviour. This perversion has always been a major cause of decline in every empire that was ever raised up in this world. It is now rampant in the UK whose empire began to decline years ago, and is accelerating now.

Male homosexual activity – as opposed to tendency – is condemned by God in serious words.

> *'If a man lies with a male as he lies with a woman, both of them have committed an abomination. They shall surely be put to death. Their blood shall be upon them.'*
>   (Leviticus 20:13)

Female lesbian activity is equally condemned.

> *'For this reason God gave them up to vile passions. For even their women exchanged the natural use for what is against nature.'*   (Romans 1:26)

Please remember that I am talking about homosexual **activity**, not homosexual **tendencies**. But homosexual behaviour is not a sickness, it is a sin. Homosexuals who say they cannot help sinning are lying. Heterosexuals are tempted to sin, just as much as homosexuals are. But they can resist temptation, so why can't homosexuals? The answer is they can, if they really want to.

Now we must love homosexuals just as we love any other sinners, but if God does not overlook their sin and perversion, then neither can we. We should heed God's severe warning to us while there is still time to escape His full anger. If the world will not listen, then let the Church listen and pray accordingly. The homosexual lobby will be among the severest persecutors of the Church in the evil days that are coming more fully soon.

Unnecessary Abortion Angers God

There are times when abortion is necessary. For example, when a mother's life is in danger during childbirth, or for some other legitimate reason. But having an abortion for the sake of convenience, or to cover up a person's immorality, angers God. He is the giver of life and He regards a human being as of tremendous value. In fact, of more value than the whole world put together. Consider what Jesus said:

> *'For what profit is it to a man if he gains the whole world and loses his own soul? Or what will a man give in exchange for his soul?'* (Matthew 16:26)

Today it is fashionable to describe a newly conceived baby as a foetus. This makes it a thing with no personality, making it easier to flush away as a piece of human debris. But God sees this and will hold those who perform unnecessary abortions, and those who ask for them, as guilty of murder. Those women who have had such abortions, but have since repented, and asked God's forgiveness for murdering their child, can be quite sure that God has forgiven them, and their crime is no longer on His records. They can be equally sure that their child is in Heaven. It goes back to the one who made it and that child has an identity in God's sight for the rest of eternity. What a wonderful comfort this can be.

The Abuse of Power Angers God

God is against tyranny, and against democracy. Scripture refers to those who lead and to those who are led. So, we do need leaders, and we do need those willing to be led. The record of history shows that there will always be leaders, and there will always be those who need to be led.

God sets high standards for leaders whether they are in the world or in the Church. But many men and women seize power in this world, and when some of them do so, their nation suffers. History is littered with such tyrants and the shameful record of their abuse of power. It stinks to the high

Heaven. Some of these evil leaders rob the nation, put their money away in secret bank accounts, they live in high style, they oppress the poor, they get whatever they want without any regard to the welfare of the nation that they are supposed to lead. God sees their abuse of power and in the great Day of Judgement they will all have to give an account of the way they have led, or misled, their nation. Nations need leaders but they must be leaders who care for those who follow them, and they must not salt away millions of pounds, which should be used for the benefit of all.

Worldly tyrants may seem to escape punishment for their abuse of power in this life, but they will never, ever, escape it in the next. They will be punished at the Great White Throne of Judgement, from which there is no escape. Church leaders who abuse their power will be punished at the Judgement Seat of Christ, which is a different aspect of God's judgement. They will be punished unless they have previously repented and made restitution down here.

> *'For we must all appear before the judgement seat of Christ, that each one may receive the things done in the body, according to what he has done, whether good or bad.'*
> (2 Corinthians 5:10)

The abuse of power is seen in the Church too, and just as God will punish worldly leaders who abuse their power, so He will punish those leaders in the Church who do likewise. Scripture forbids tyranny:

> *'...nor as being lords over those entrusted to you, but being examples to the flock.'*	(1 Peter 5:3)

The Bible condemns tyrrany, but it does not suggest democracy either. The 'voice of the people' seems to be a good principle, but it can easily lead to anarchy or, at least, constant argument. Scripture advocates voluntary submission to good leaders.

> *'Remember those who rule over you, who have spoken the word of God to you, whose faith follow, considering the outcome of their conduct.'*	(Hebrews 13:7)

The Love and Misuse of Money Angers God

Money is not evil, it is necessary. It can be a good thing. God is not against money, He owns it all, He invented it.

> ' "The silver is Mine, and the gold is Mine," says the LORD of hosts.' (Haggai 2:8)

It is the **love** of money that angers God, not the possession of it.

> 'For the love of money is a root of all kinds of evil, for which some have strayed from the faith in their greediness, and pierced themselves through with many sorrows.'
> (1 Timothy 6:10)

The love of money comes from the awful covetousness, which afflicts most of mankind.

> 'You shall burn the carved images of their gods with fire; you shall not covet the silver or gold that is on them, nor take it for yourselves, lest you be snared by it; for it is an abomination to the LORD your God.' (Deuteronomy 7:25)

An offshoot of this love of money and covetousness is the frantic pursuit of interest today. The scene in the average money market must be a stink in the nostrils of God. The frantic bargaining, howling and screaming into telephones, and going berserk in case they miss the opportunity of adding a tiny increase in interest. God regards it as extortion.

> ' "In you they take bribes to shed blood; you take usury and increase; you have made profit from your neighbours by extortion, and have forgotten Me," says the LORD GOD.'
> (Ezekiel 22:12)

These sins of the love of money and covetousness undoubtedly bring the anger of God to bear.

But the misuse of money is not confined to the world. It is seen in the Church too. Some church leaders in the UK use the scripture 'Bring all the tithes into the storehouse', as a way of making sure that the people's offerings are used for the schemes which these leaders want to bring about. Some want huge buildings, and some might want them for legitimate

reasons, but others want them in order to show off. Some
leaders have pet projects and they are determined to see
them through, and they merely use the church's offerings as
a means of satisfying their own ambitions. Now some
schemes may well be of the Lord, but some that I have seen
are very suspect. Leaders have to be very, very careful that
they don't fall into the sin of the unrighteous love of money.

God is not more angry with the world's love of money
than He is angry with the Church's love of money. When it
comes to sin and His punishment of this sin, He is no
respecter of persons:

> '...God shows no partiality.'   (Acts 10:34)

Denominationalism Angers God

I do not think that God is troubled about denominations,
but He hates 'denominationalism', which is described in
Scripture as 'factions', 'party spirit', 'elitism'.

> '...for you are still carnal. For where there are envy, strife,
> and divisions among you, are you not carnal and behaving
> like mere men? For when one says, "I am of Paul," and
> another, "I am of Apollos," are you not carnal?'
>
> (1 Corinthians 3:3–4)

God actually uses denominations to keep certain truths
alive. The Baptists stress the **truth of baptism**, The Method-
ists stress the **truth of holiness**, or at least they used to. The
Brethren stress the **voracity of the Bible**, the Pentecostals
stress the **work of the Holy Spirit** and so on. But God hates it
when we are splitting 'doctrinal hairs' and excommunicating
each other when we don't toe their party line. This is the sin
of denominationalism.

Suppression of the Truth Angers God

Many preachers are guilty of this. They prefer to preach the
nice things that please congregations or conference dele-
gates. But things such as the anger of God, the fear of God,
His demands for holiness, the penalties of disobedience to

God's laws, are not on the agenda of many of these conferences, nor in the preaching syllabuses in the majority of our churches. The suppression of these aspects of God's truth makes them guilty before God, and if they do not change they will have to give an account of their suppression of these truths in the great Day of Judgement. On that day the whole world will be terrified by an angry God, so much so that as I wrote before, they will try to hide from him (Revelation 6:16).

As David Pawson says, 'Judgement then becomes not general, but personal.' So Christian preachers may not be in the second resurrection, where the unsaved are judged, but they will have to give their account at the first resurrection, the Judgement Seat of Christ. Populist preaching gathers the crowds and entertains the Church, but it does not fit them for rugged discipleship and holy warfare.

Mocking the Messengers of God Angers God

God, in His grace, has sent one messenger after another into this world to bring the message that the anger of God can be avoided. But, although many have listened, and escaped the final penalty, so many people have not. The remedy is still available, but for how long?

> *'But they mocked the messengers of God, despised His words, and scoffed at His prophets, until the wrath of the Lord arose against His people, till there was no remedy.'*
>
> (2 Chronicles 36:16)

David Pawson is a messenger who is often ignored or avoided, and yet he is one of the most powerful prophetic teachers I know. Apart from him, or me, I do not know many who proclaim the unpopular doctrines as faithfully.

Profaning the Sabbath is Sin Against God

Whether we regard Saturday or Sunday as the Sabbath, it is important to regard one day in seven as devoted to the Lord. It need not be a dull or miserable day, it can be a day of rejoicing in God's goodness and a day of godly relaxation.

'Remember the Sabbath day, to keep it holy.'

(Exodus 20:8)

Israel suffered for its disobedience to this commandment of God and so have other nations. The country previously known as the USSR once abolished Sunday, saying it was unnecessary. After a short while they discovered that production was down, more shoddy work came out of the industries, more people were sick, morale plunged to an all-time low. So, they had to reinstate Sunday.

'Did not your fathers do thus, and did not our God bring all this disaster on us and on this city? Yet you bring added wrath on Israel by profaning the Sabbath.'

(Nehemiah 13:18)

Is the UK immune to God's anger? After all, it does profane the Sabbath or Sunday, so why should we be free of God's judgement on our profanity? So, if we ignore God's day in order to shop more conveniently with Sunday trading, we must bear the consequences.

Here are some more things that anger God:

Murmuring

Murmuring, or grumbling, does not seem to be an awful sin, it is the order of the day in most countries. What would the British do if they couldn't complain about the weather? But when we realise how good God is to us, it is an insult to His grace to grumble. After all, most of us are fed and housed. It also arouses His anger.

'Now when the people complained, it displeased the LORD; for the LORD heard it, and His anger was aroused. So the fire of the LORD burned among them, and consumed some in the outskirts of the camp.'   (Numbers 11:1)

Jealousy

Jealousy is a powerful thing. It can lead to murder and robbery, it causes splits in churches and families, and coups in nations. Because it has such disastrous effects it arouses the anger of God.

> *'So they said, "Has the* Lord *indeed spoken only through Moses? Has He not spoken through us also?" And the* Lord *heard it.'*   (Numbers 12:2)

Pause for a minute to think. Are you jealous of anybody? In your church? Do you wish that you had their job? Are you murmuring? Do you constantly grumble? If any of these things are found in our heart, let's take warning, the anger of God is aroused by these things.

Unbelief

Unbelief, whether it is found in ancient Israel or in the modern world, is regarded seriously by God. Those who jeer at the Bible and do not believe it are in serious danger.

> *'Do not be deceived, God is not mocked; for whatever a man sows, that he will also reap.'*   (Galatians 6:7)

In the Judgement Day all unbelievers and scoffers will be judged by the things in the very book that they laughed and jeered at.

> *'And I saw the dead, small and great, standing before God, and books were opened. And another book was opened, which is the Book of Life. And the dead were judged according to their works, by the things which were written in the books.'*   (Revelation 20:12)

Unbelief is infectious. Some men in the Old Testament, who were unbelieving, were virtually guilty of murder because many of their fellows died because of their unbelief and cowardice. You may remember the story when the spies were sent out by Joshua to see if the land could be taken. As some of them came back with unbelief they moaned:

> *'But the men who had gone up with him said, "We are not able to go up against the people, for they are stronger than we."'*   (Numbers 13:31)

They infected the rest of the people through their unbelief.

They suffered for it. Not one of them ever entered into the Promised Land.

There are also many, many ways in which we can arouse the anger of God. Greed, witchcraft, including horoscopes, which are some of the most insidious and destructive things around, and yet found in most newspapers and magazines today. These horoscopes are not a bit of fun, they are delusions of the devil.

Other things that arouse the anger of God are selfishness, drunkenness and covetousness, to name but a few more. Scripture warns us against them all.

> *'... idolatry, sorcery, hatred, contentions, jealousies, outbursts of wrath, selfish ambitions, dissensions, heresies, envy, murders, drunkenness, revelries, and the like; of which I tell you beforehand, just as I also told you in time past, that those who practice such things will not inherit the kingdom of God.'*   (Galatians 5:20–21)

If anyone persists in any of these sins, that is if they become habitual, and people do not repent of them but allow these things to possess their being, they will never enter Heaven. This is clearly stated:

> *'But the cowardly, unbelieving, abominable, murderers, sexually immoral, sorcerers, idolaters, and all liars shall have their part in the lake which burns with fire and brimstone, which is the second death.'*   (Revelation 21:8)

But, here is a wonderful thing. Even to those who are guilty of any of the above sins, God still makes an appeal:

> *'... while it is said:*
>   *"Today, if you will hear His voice,*
>   *Do not harden your hearts as in the rebellion."'*
>   (Hebrews 3:15)

This is not the word of an angry and implacable God who shows no mercy, it is a cry from an angry but compassionate God. It is a word straight out of His heart. In any word from God, be it ever so scathing, there are always the undertones of love and the overtones of grace. If a word from God, such as a prophecy, does not contain these things, it is not the word of God. God is angry, but God is also merciful.

In closing this chapter I want to say it is surely madness to reject His mercy, it is madness to risk His anger. Let us turn from these things, these causes of God's anger, let them not even be named among us, and if we are guilty of them let us speedily repent, run to God and find forgiveness from sin and delivery from His anger.

Chapter 6

God's Anger Was Expressed at Calvary

With so many things causing God to be angry, it was inevitable that He would have to express it. He did so at Calvary, where He expressed it totally, and without any mercy toward Jesus. His anger fell upon Jesus who became our substitute. There was no mercy at all for Him, no grace extended to Him, but there was abundant mercy extended to us because Jesus bore the weight of God's anger for our sin.

Usually the Expression of God's Anger is Mercifully Brief

The Bible says so:

> 'For His anger is **but for a moment**,
> His favour **is for life**;
> Weeping may endure for a night,
> But joy comes in the morning.'   (Psalm 30:5)

God shows that His anger does not abolish His love and mercy when He says to a sinful nation which is under His judgement:

> 'For a mere moment I have forsaken you,
> But with great mercies I will gather you.'   (Isaiah 54:7)

The nation was Israel, under severe judgement because of its constant sin. The anger of God was poured out against it.

But it does not invalidate His mercy. When the scripture says, *'For a brief moment was I angry'*, the word 'brief' is relative. A nation or an individual may experience God's anger for a considerable time. For example, Israel bore anger for 40 years in the wilderness. But, we have to remember that God's time scale is different from ours.

> *'For a thousand years in Your sight are like yesterday when it is past,*
> *And like a watch in the night.'*   (Psalm 90:4)

So, usually, whether it seems a long time or not, God's anger is fairly brief, except for the most terrible time of all.

In the case of Jesus, God's anger was poured out for a comparatively short time, a matter of hours, in fact. But, it was poured out without any restraint, the whole burden of God's wrath fell upon Jesus. It was at Calvary's Cross that God showed His fierce anger to the ultimate degree, and there was no relief from it for the one who hung upon it, Jesus, as He bore, on our behalf, the fierce anger of an offended deity. He did this so that we could be delivered from it.

It Was God the Father Who Put His Son to Death

He was not really murdered. He surrendered Himself to God who then allowed Him to be killed – for us. The Bible says that God smote Him using human agencies.

> *'Surely He has borne our griefs and carried our sorrows;*
> *Yet we esteemed Him stricken, smitten by God, and afflicted.'*   (Isaiah 53:4)

Despite the terrible task of pouring out His anger on Jesus, God did not hesitate because He loved us so dearly.

> *'He who did not spare His own Son, but delivered Him up for us all, how shall He not with Him also freely give us all things?'*   (Romans 8:32)

God is a God of judgement, which means making a decision or issuing a verdict based on the evidence. That is judgement. God is also a God of justice, and justice means the execution of what is right. In Scripture the words are often combined. Now in order to be such a God, He had to enforce this judgement and justice. In no way could He pervert it. He had to fulfil judgement and justice.

> *'Does God subvert judgement?*
> *Or does the Almighty pervert justice?*   (Job 8:3)

Sinners had broken the royal law of God and they had to be punished for their crime. If God had ignored sin and not demanded justice, He could no longer have been a holy, just and righteous God. He would have failed. He would have been imperfect. Therefore He had to execute justice, even when the one upon whom the sentence fell was Jesus His own Son.

God could not have punished an ordinary man for the world's sin because He could not find one who was perfect. The one who could become the unspotted sacrifice, which righteousness demanded, was not to be found in mankind. Nor could God find a man who was willing to be made the sole culprit for the sin of the whole world.

Jesus was the only man who was qualified, and He was the only one who offered Himself to God for this purpose. John realised this when He said:

> *'The next day John saw Jesus coming toward him, and said, "Behold! The Lamb of God who takes away the sin of the world!"'*   (John 1:29)

Never forget that Jesus suffered, not for His own sin because He never sinned, but He suffered for us. We are the ones who sinned and broke God's law.

> *'All we like sheep have gone astray; we have turned, every one, to his own way; and the LORD has laid on Him the iniquity of us all.'*   (Isaiah 53:6)

John Stott says,

> 'Christ died our death when He died for our sins.'

Christ did not only die in order to pay the penalty for the sins we committed, but He died because of our basic sin –

the fact that we were hopelessly tainted with sin when we were born. We were born with this fatal disease called sin, and this is what the theologians call 'total depravity'. The Bible points out that we were born in sin in Psalm 51:5.

God forsook His Son. He did not do so while Jesus walked with His Father on earth, but only when Jesus was made sin for us on the Cross. Then the Father had no option. He had to forsake His Son because Jesus became unbearably horrible in His sight, as He became the very essence of sin.

I often try to think about the agony of the Father as He turned away from His Son. I also try to share something of the pain of the Spirit as He also had to depart from the life of the One who had never grieved Him. God the Holy Spirit took Jesus as far as He could before leaving Him. Then, at the Cross the Spirit could no longer walk with Jesus, because they were no longer 'agreed'.

> *'Do two walk together unless they have agreed to do so?'*
> (Amos 3:3)

So, both Father and Spirit left Him.

> *'About the ninth hour Jesus cried out in a loud voice, ... "My God, my God, why have you forsaken me?"'*
> (Matthew 27:46)

This was the moment of agony unparalleled in the history of the Creation.

Jesus died. The Bible says He died.

> *'And when Jesus had cried out again in a loud voice, He gave up His spirit.'* (Matthew 27:50)

Again:

> *'With a loud cry, Jesus breathed His last.'* (Mark 15:37)

Some critics say that Jesus swooned: the disciples stole His body – they hallucinated – it was fraud – it was myth. Such critics are best ignored.

Jesus entered into Hell. The Athanasian Creed says that Jesus descended into Hell, and I have no reason to doubt it. He suffered on our behalf, the fate of all who had offended against God's laws and never repented. The fate of these is to be separated from God forever and to be under His anger.

Some people might say that if God's anger was completely vented at Calvary, then there should not be any manifestation of His anger today. Yes, God did pour out His complete anger at the Cross, but the benefits of the Cross only become effective for those who are born again: those who receive deliverance from God's anger as an act of their will. If they do not, the anger and the judgement of God hangs over them until they repent. If they don't, it hangs over them forever.

Why did Jesus die in our place? Firstly, because His Father asked Him to. Secondly, because He loved us enough to do it in order to save us from the anger of God and eternal damnation.

> *'Much more then, having now been justified by His blood, we shall be saved from wrath through Him.'*   (Romans 5:9)

Remember the grief of God at Calvary and never make the Cross cheap.

Chapter 7

God's Anger Is Expressed Today

God's Anger Is Slow to Be Roused

Having said that God's anger was expressed at Calvary, I now want to enlarge on the fact that God's anger is expressed today. As I have said, God's anger is slow to be roused. All through the centuries God has been patient with sinners. Mankind has sinned and continually flouted His laws. They have continuously and willingly turned against God. They have laughed at His Word, they have rejected His preachers and prophets, they have persecuted those messengers of God and they have persecuted God's people. Many times God reached out to mankind, but He was rejected so often:

> *'God, who at various times and in various ways spoke in time past to the fathers by the prophets.'* (Hebrews 1:1)

They have consistently rejected God and turned to their own enjoyment. Their motto is:

> *'...Let us eat and drink, for tomorrow we die!'*
>
> (Isaiah 22:13)

Despite all this continual rejection, despite men and women flouting His laws century after century, God has been very patient and actually restrained His anger.

> *'...when once the Divine longsuffering waited in the days of Noah, while the ark was being prepared, in which a few, that is, eight souls, were saved through water.'* (1 Peter 3:20)

God has to deal drastically with sinful people as He did in the great flood. But, the scripture shows how reluctant He is to do so until it is absolutely necessary.

> *'The Lord is not slack concerning His promise, as some count slackness, but is longsuffering toward us, not willing that any should perish but that all should come to repentance.'*
>
> (2 Peter 3:9)

Here again, God's anger is balanced by His patient love and compassion. As the scripture says:

> *'But You, O Lord, are a God full of compassion, and gracious,*
> *Longsuffering and abundant in mercy and truth.'*
>
> (Psalm 86:15)

God is slow to anger, but anger is there within Him. There are times when He even commanded Moses, that great intercessor, to stop praying for the nation. He says:

> *'Now therefore, let Me alone, that My wrath may burn hot against them and I may consume them. And I will make of you a great nation.'* (Exodus 32:10)

God became so incensed with the nation of Israel's deliberate and awful sin that He had to express His anger. And yet, He stopped short of absolute destruction. You see, His anger never invalidates His compassion. Scripture shows this:

> *'But He, **being full of compassion**, forgave their iniquity,*
> *And did not destroy them.*
> *Yes, many a time He turned His anger away,*
> *And did not stir up all His wrath.'* (Psalm 78:38)

God's Anger Is Fierce When it Is Expressed

It was expressed against God's own nation of Israel. Its priests knew exactly what they should do, and what they should not do. For example, they knew there was only one way to use incense in the temple worship, and they also knew whose particular work it was to offer it to God. So God was justified in judging them severely when they disobeyed His commandments as in this scripture:

> 'Then Nadab and Abihu, the sons of Aaron, each took his censer and put fire in it, put incense on it, and offered profane fire before the LORD, which He had not commanded them.'   (Leviticus 10:1)

Why should we feel sorry for those who knowingly and deliberately break God's laws? The modern counterpart of offering false fire, or offering wrong incense, can be offering shoddy worship to God in our churches. And there is a lot of that about. If our hearts are not pure, our worship stinks in the nostrils of God, it does not rise as a sweet savour in His nostrils.

Partial obedience is another aspect of modern disobedience to the laws of God. God looks for complete and willing obedience to His laws, not just obedience to a few when it suits us. Partial obedience is not complete, is not God-honouring, is not what it ought to be, and just as the anger of God was fierce when He saw wrong behaviour in His nation of Israel, He is equally fierce when He sees wrong behaviour in His Church today.

His Anger Was Expressed Against Israel's Enemies

God can be quite ruthless when necessary, as He was when destroying the Amalekites, as I previously said (1 Samuel 15:2–3).

It could seem that God was cruel to destroy a whole nation, including supposedly innocent women and children. However, God foresaw that the children would grow up to be just as wicked and cruel as their parents were. He saw that they would harm His nation of Israel so, in His mercy to Israel, He poured out His fierce anger on the Amalekites.

It Is Expressed Against the Nations in the Last Days

There is a day in God's diary that will never be erased from it. It is the Great Day of His Judgement of the world. At that time the Anti-Christ will mobilise all the nations against Israel to destroy it, but then, God will pour out all His fierce anger against the Anti-Christ and the nations and will destroy them.

> *'Now out of His mouth goes a sharp sword, that with it He should strike the nations. And He Himself will rule them with a rod of iron. He Himself treads the winepress of the fierceness and wrath of Almighty God.'* (Revelation 19:15)

In this scripture is mentioned a *'rod of iron'*, and this rod of iron can mean a straight edge or a ruler. In that day, God will measure up all people against His standard of righteousness. Those who measure up, having attained righteousness from Jesus, will go into Heaven. Those who do not measure up will never enter Heaven but will enter into Hell eternally.

It Is Expressed Against His Own Church When it Sins or Becomes Impure

Jesus wants His Church to be a pure Bride not a spotty harlot. Our Father wants His family to be clean, holy, and obedient. So, when necessary He applies discipline to that end.

> *'For whom the LORD loves He chastens, and scourges every son whom He receives.'* (Hebrews 12:6)

God is not afraid to take away His saints if it is necessary for discipline, such as Ananias and Sapphira.

> *'But a certain man named Ananias, with Sapphira his wife, sold a possession. And he kept back part of the proceeds, his wife also being aware of it, and brought a certain part and laid it at the apostles' feet. But Peter said, "Ananias, why has Satan filled your heart to lie to the Holy Spirit and keep back part of the price of the land for yourself? While it remained, was it not your own? And after it was sold, was it not in your own control? Why have you conceived this thing in your heart? You have not lied to men but to God." Then Ananias, hearing these words, fell down and breathed his last. So great fear came upon all those who heard these things. And the young men arose and wrapped him up,*

carried him out, and buried him. Now it was about three hours later when his wife came in, not knowing what had happened. And Peter answered her, "Tell me whether you sold the land for so much?" She said, "Yes, for so much." Then Peter said to her, "How is it that you have agreed together to test the Spirit of the Lord? Look, the feet of those who have buried your husband are at the door, and they will carry you out."' (Acts 5:1–9)

I don't believe that these two disciples lost their salvation, even though they lost their lives. But what a shame that they lost their chance to extend the Kingdom on the earth. If only they had been truthful to the Holy Spirit, they could have lived on and extended the Kingdom and laid up more treasure in Heaven. What a tragedy they didn't do it. By the way, have you lied to the Holy Spirit? Are you in danger of God's wrath? I wonder.

Why does God discipline His people so severely? My answer is, so that we become holy. God's great intention is for His people to become like His Son, which is our great destiny. Just as God had to discipline His people Israel, sometimes by drastic measures, so God disciplines His people today for the same reason. He must have a holy Church. He must have a Church that loves Him and knows Him.

God's Anger Has to Be Expressed for Several Reasons

So that righteousness is established

Without righteousness and valid standards of behaviour, the world would be in total anarchy and total chaos. We have to have standards and they have to be righteous standards. Unrighteousness is sin and it degrades us. When a nation turns away from God it becomes degraded, and that nation bears the consequences of brushing aside righteousness, as unrighteousness takes its place.

The Scriptures point out that all unrighteousness is sin.

'All unrighteousness is sin, and there is sin not leading to death.' (1 John 5:17)

But righteousness is good and uplifting.

> *'Righteousness exalts a nation,*
> *But sin is a reproach to any people.'*   (Proverbs 14:34)

There must be standards of behaviour if the world is not to plunge into complete chaos, and God has provided these standards in His laws. But we also need a way to enforce these standards. If national leaders will not do so because they, like the rest of us, have a bias towards sin, then the Church must enforce those standards – or, at least display their obedience to them. But God will enforce His standards of righteousness one day because He will fulfil His desire for a righteous world, and His desire will be fulfilled in the great day.

So that evil is restrained

God's reaction towards sin causes Him to restrain sin and lawlessness. He does so in several ways. Mostly, through the powerful person of the Holy Spirit. His work of restraining evil is found in the Bible.

> *'For the mystery of lawlessness is already at work; only He who now restrains will do so until He is taken out of the way.'*   (2 Thessalonians 2:7)

But God also restrains sin by another way, by instituting the Church, which is meant to be salt and light in this world. Salt prevents corruption and encourages growth in crops. Light demolishes darkness.

In addition, God restrains the devil. Satan can only do what God allows Him to do. He is, in the last analysis, only a servant who must do what God says. When Satan wanted to kill Job because he was a righteous man, God gave Satan a measure of freedom to try to distress him, but He did set boundaries around Job's life, thus restraining the devil and thus retaining the life of His servant.

God's anger, which causes Him to restrain sin, is evidence of His mercy to the righteous. Sin would be absolutely rampant if God did not restrain it at all. A non-angry God would just have let everything go and the result would be chaos.

God's anger causes Him to react against evil. It might not seem that He does, judging by the prevalence of evil in this world. But He does so much restraining that is unseen by most of us. We cannot see gravity but it is working, and that is a restraint, it restrains things onto the earth, it keeps them down on the earth. God could be more severe than He is, as in the past when He flooded the whole world. And, of course, He will be again when He cleanses the earth by fire. That is very severe. But, at this moment His anger is tempered with mercy. Let those who need it, run to God find it while the going is good.

So that sin is judged

All sins bring judgement on us. If God did not judge sin by expressing His anger He could not be righteous because He would not have dealt justly with man's disobedience. God does not recognise degrees of sin, to Him all sin is sin. If people persist in these sins, they will experience the anger of God forever. Let me say again, it is not worth the risk, let us run from the judgement of God while we can.

For sin to be restrained and for justice to be done, there must be a power which is above those who perpetrate injustice. Most countries have a judicial system in order to restrain injustice in their nation. Certainly some abuse their powers, but the principle still remains, we need a system to restrain evil. The laws have to be enforced by the exercise of power and severity. When it is enforced, the authorities in the nations mirror the severity – the righteous severity and judgement of God. God's anger is always a just anger for it is based on His perfect assessment of every situation.

So that sin is seen to be judged

If there were no obvious signs of God's judgement in the world, there would be no visible justice. Mankind would be at the mercy of the unlawful. Just laws are good, but ineffective if no one ever enforces them. There would be no deterrent. Because God's anger is apparent in this world, there is a deterrent. Sin is seen to be judged, even in our day.

So that the principle of punishment is shown

If God did not get angry, punishment would never be enforced, it would never be seen to be enforced. So, He has to reveal His punishment. Punishment today is a dirty word, it has been replaced by tolerance. We are told that if we were more tolerant, criminals would not be so eager to commit their crimes. But God is intolerant, He metes out punishment for crimes. Actually, punishment is a teaching method. How does a child learn right from wrong unless there is severe treatment sometimes? And just as parents have to be severe on occasions in order to teach their children, God is severe sometimes because He wants to teach the world the difference between right and wrong, and the danger of punishment for sin, just as parents teach their children.

So that God does not harbour His anger

Scripture assures us that He will never retain His anger forever, or bear grudges against mankind.

> *He will not always strive with us,*
> *Nor will He keep His anger forever.'*   (Psalm 103:9)

Now if we, as human beings, harbour our anger, we eventually become bitter. That is why we must learn to express it, to get rid of it, so that we don't become bitter. Now our friends, or our spouses, may not be able to cope with our anger if we do harbour it. But, fortunately, we can express it to God and be done with it. If we express it to our friends they may not be able to cope, but we can express it to God quite safely because He can cope. This is quite a scriptural occupation:

> *'I pour out my complaint before Him;*
> *I declare before Him my trouble.'*   (Psalm 142:2)

God does get angry, and He restrains His anger for a while, but in the meantime, He does not become bitter. If He did, He would be harbouring sin within him, and obviously this is impossible.

His Anger Is Expressed Today

God shows His anger now, even before the great Day of Judgement. He gives timely reminders on earth that He is not a God to be trifled with. If only people would understand this. We must not think that every earthly tragedy is an expression of God's anger, but when Israel continuously sinned against God, He did show His anger against them:

> *'He cast on them the fierceness of His anger,*
> *Wrath, indignation, and trouble,*
> *By sending angels of destruction among them.'*
>
> (Psalm 78:49)

Although God does express His anger, He doesn't do everything personally. He uses His angels to do His work for Him sometimes. So, angelic powers apply God's anger when He directs them to do so. All angels, whether good or evil, are under His control. When He sends them, they go, when He doesn't send them, they stay. The ungodly cannot escape the effects of God's anger, and sometimes the righteous suffer with the unrighteous as God pours out His righteous anger on this world today.

But it is important to see that God does not delight in bringing tragedy into the world. He does not dole out disasters with malicious glee, in fact, He doesn't cause tragedy at all, He only allows it. Sinful men cause tragedy by their inhumanity to their fellows. War was invented in Hell, not in Heaven. Murder was unknown until sin entered the world. God gets blamed for all kinds of troubles, but it is mankind, aided and abetted by the devil, which is the root cause of tragedy in this world.

Certainly God allows trouble to happen, but it is very different from saying that He causes it. For example, some of the following circumstances in the world are due to man's misuse of the earth, and God utilises this to punish them for their sin. Here in the following section are ways in which God allows His anger to be expressed through the stupidity of men.

Droughts

God does not cause drought, but He allows it to happen if people ignore His laws and His principles. Droughts are usually the result of man's misuse of the earth. If people insist on chopping down trees, then the unprotected earth will turn to dust and cease to be cultivated. The Sahara Desert was once the bread basket of the Roman Empire.

On other occasions God allows droughts in order to show His anger as in:

> '... *lest the Lord's anger be aroused against you, and He shut up the heavens so that there be no rain, and the land yield no produce, and you perish quickly from the good land which the* Lord *is giving you.'* (Deuteronomy 11:17)

Displacement

If a nation ignores God's repeated warnings, He will operate in justice such as uprooting the nations and banishing them elsewhere. This is seen in:

> '*And the* Lord *uprooted them from their land in anger, in wrath, and in great indignation, and cast them into another land, as it is this day.'* (Deuteronomy 29:28)

However, these manifestations of His anger are only the foretaste of His anger on the earth. In the Day of Judgement God's anger will be poured fully and finally on all who have disobeyed Him.

No wonder the Bible urges us to '... *flee from the wrath to come'* (Luke 3:7). The Bible points us to Jesus as the only saviour from the wrath of God. Christians are invited to look for His coming. The purpose in God's anger is not to destroy, but to save. He does not want to destroy the sinner, but the power of sin that enslaves us. Jesus can rescue us, but only if we surrender to His Lordship and experience the new birth. Why not let Him do so while we are alive? At all costs let's run to Him while we can.

The Value of God's Anger

Imagine a world where there was no restraining of evil, no judgement for the oppressed, no punishment of crime, anarchy, and with chaos prevailing. Crime would be rampant, greed would flourish, the strong would crush the weak. Murder, genocide, cruelty and violence would be the order of the day. Many people would say that this situation exists now, and this is true, but if there were no restraint at all, it would be far, far worse in the world. God's anger is valuable because it causes Him to curb the evil one in the world.

This is the kind of world that Satan, God's enemy, is determined to have, and he could have it with the help of those who are determined sinners, and the anarchists among them. However, he will never actually do it because of the expressed anger of God, which brings the restraint of evil.

Chapter 8

God's Anger Is Expressed at Judgement Day

I have said that God's anger was expressed at Calvary. It is expressed in our day, and it will be expressed in the future at the Judgement Day.

The word 'judgement' can be very easily misunderstood today, but judgement includes vengeance, avenging and justice. Judgement means a 'decision or a verdict based on all the evidence'. And judgement, perfect judgement, will be meted out on the day of wrath. Everyone who has ever been born or created will be there. It is the Judgement of the Great White Throne of which I speak, mentioned in Revelation

> *'Then I saw a great white throne and Him who sat on it, from whose face the earth and the heaven fled away. And there was found no place for them.'* (Revelation 20:11)

Justice means 'what is right', or the 'execution of what is right'. When Jesus comes He will execute what is right.

> *'He will not fail nor be discouraged,*
> *Till He has established justice in the earth;*
> *and the coastlands shall wait for His law.'* (Isaiah 42:4)

The world will then see what God means by judgement, justice and vengeance. Jesus will enforce all these things. By the way, 'vengeance' means, 'that which proceeds out of justice'. The Greek words means 'vindication', 'retribution', 'repayment'.

But God's vengeance, unlike man's, is free from vindictiveness. Scripture does not portray a malicious Jesus intent on mere revenge, but One who comes to do that which is merited by those who reject Him. Jesus will come, as the Bible says:

> *'... in flaming fire taking vengeance on those who do not know God, and on those who do not obey the gospel of our Lord Jesus Christ.'* (2 Thessalonians 1:8)

There is a day in God's diary, as I have said before, and it is irrecoverably fixed there. No one can alter it, or erase it. And the Bible declares this:

> *'... because He has appointed a day on which He will judge the world in righteousness by the Man whom He has ordained. He has given assurance of this to all by raising Him from the dead.'* (Acts 17:31)

And again in

> *'And as it is appointed for men to die once, but after this the judgment.'* (Hebrews 9:27)

If men can continually return to their sin deliberately and persistently, God can return to being angry again with them, continually.

In the Judgement Day all those who follow the devil will join Satan in hell, the place of eternal absence from God. The face of an angry God will be so terrible at that time that people will cry out for something to blot out the sight.

> *'... and said to the mountains and rocks, "Fall on us and hide us from the face of Him who sits on the throne and from the wrath of the Lamb!"'* (Revelation 6:16)

This is His eternal judgement to which God has condemned Satan, together with all who side with him. Judgement Day is the occasion in which God will pour out His anger once and for all on the unbelieving world. At the moment, as my friend David Pawson puts it, His anger is simmering, but on that day it will boil over.

No One Escapes This Judgement Day

Just as no one escapes death or resurrection, so no one escapes this day. There will be no hiding place to escape to. The Bible is very accurate about this:

> *'But why do you judge your brother? Or why do you show contempt for your brother? For we shall all stand before the judgment seat of Christ, for it is written:*
>
> *"As I live, says the LORD,*
> *Every knee shall bow to Me,*
> *And every tongue shall confess to God."*
>
> *So then each of us shall give account of himself to God.'*
>
> (Romans 14:10–12)

How can anybody evade God? The Psalmist points out the impossibility of doing so.

> *'Where can I go from Your Spirit?*
> *Or where can I flee from Your presence?'*   (Psalm 139:7)

Judgement will be meted out to everyone at the Throne of God. All the unsaved dead will stand there:

> *'And I saw the dead, small and great, standing before God, and books were opened. And another book was opened, which is the Book of Life. And the dead were judged according to their works, by the things which were written in the books.'*   (Revelation 20:12)

Only One Question

I believe that God will only need to ask one question of those who stand before Him on that day. I think it might well be, 'What did you do with My Son Jesus?' That is the pivotal question to all mankind both now and then.

The Day of God's Anger

This is the time when God's anger is poured out as the Bible says in Revelation 6:16.

The Judge on that day is Jesus

'For the Father judges no one, but has committed all judgment to the Son.' (John 5:22)

He is the One appointed to judge the whole world:

'... in the day when God will judge the secrets of men by Jesus Christ, according to my gospel.' (Romans 2:16)

The same Jesus who was judged for our sin, is now the Judge of those who rejected the salvation which He accomplished for mankind at Calvary. Those being judged will be all those who rejected Jesus as their Saviour, either deliberately or by neglect. Jesus grieved greatly over their rejection while He was on the earth. Some of them were Israelites to whom He said:

'O Jerusalem, Jerusalem, the one who kills the prophets and stones those who are sent to her! How often I wanted to gather your children together, as a hen gathers her chicks under her wings, but you were not willing!'

(Matthew 23:37)

He wanted them so much in His Kingdom: His heart went out to them in love and desire, but, at the same time, He made the consequences of their rejection very clear.

'He who believes in the Son has everlasting life; and He who does not believe the Son shall not see life, but the wrath of God abides on him.' (John 3:36)

He spoke the words of life to all mankind, and their response to that word decides the issue in the great day.

'He who rejects Me, and does not receive My words, has that which judges him; the word that I have spoken will judge him in the last day.' (John 12:48)

There is no-one to speak on behalf of the wicked on Judgement Day

They could have had an advocate while they were alive on earth to plead on their behalf, Jesus. But they refused Him. Now they cannot have His help. While they were alive, some of the wicked refused His help and they did it deliberately, and yet God still said to them:

> *'I have stretched out My hands all day long to a rebellious*
>   *people,*
> *Who walk in a way that is not good,*
> *According to their own thoughts.'*   (Isaiah 65:2)

Sadly God had to say:

> *'But you are not willing to come to Me that you may have*
> *life.'*   (John 5:40)

Others refused His help by neglect. They just never got round to reading the Bible, or if they did so, they did not cry out for His help. How sad that such people had the Bible, had a chance, refused it and now have to bear the anger of God!

Only One Verdict

Seeing that this occasion is the judgement of the ungodly, there is only one verdict at this throne – damnation, or as modern versions put it, condemnation. This verdict is a terrible one. Having separated the godly from the ungodly among the nations, God will utter His final verdict to the ungodly.

> *'... "Depart from Me, you cursed, into the everlasting fire*
> *prepared for the devil and his angels." '*   (Matthew 25:41)

The verdict has an eternal effect according to Scripture:

> *'He who is unjust, let him be unjust still; he who is filthy, let*
> *him be filthy still; he who is righteous, let him be righteous*
> *still; he who is holy, let him be holy still.'*
>
> (Revelation 22:11)

Some believe in annihilation. Their theory is that when we are dead, we are done for and that's it. I do not believe in annihilation, I have to believe what I think Jesus plainly taught about eternal torment. I don't like this doctrine. I shudder at it, but I have to preach it. I write more on this matter in my book *Heaven and Hell*, published by Sovereign World.

Ungodly people will be set forever in the mould which they adopted in their earthly life. God's verdict is a fair one. He simply repays the ungodly and He does it without spite. He cannot do otherwise. But all God really does is to confirm the decision, which the unsaved made in their lifetime.

God's Anger Will Be Expressed in Full ...

I have said before that God is slow to get angry, but when He does, His anger is fierce. John's end-time vision in Revelation shows this.

Jesus is far from the 'gentle Jesus, meek and mild' mentioned in an old, sentimental chorus. He is seen in Scripture as a man of war, enforcing the rule of God and revealing His fierce anger.

> *'Now out of His mouth goes a sharp sword, that with it He should strike the nations. And He Himself will rule them with a rod of iron. He Himself treads the winepress of the fierceness and wrath of Almighty God.'* (Revelation 19:15)

The anger of God is unstoppable, no one will be able to stand against it.

> *'For the great day of His wrath has come, and who is able to stand?'*   (Revelation 6:17)

God's anger on that day is without mercy. Now we are in the age of grace, but there will come a time when mercy is not to be found at all, at the Judgement Seat of God.

Even in earlier times people were judged without mercy.

> *'Anyone who has rejected Moses' law dies without mercy on the testimony of two or three witnesses. Of how much worse punishment, do you suppose, will he be thought worthy who has trampled the Son of God underfoot, counted the blood of the covenant by which He was sanctified a common thing, and insulted the Spirit of grace?'*   (Hebrews 10:28–29)

The words in the scripture, '... who has trampled the Son of God underfoot', referred to people who, in their lifetime, have done this. They cannot expect mercy on Judgement Day.

Trample the Son now, bow before Him then as Judge. And on that day there is no mercy at all to be found for the unsaved.

... and Complete

God's Judgement is wholly righteous.

> *'Then I saw another sign in heaven, great and marvelous: seven angels having the seven last plagues, for in them the wrath of God is complete.'* (Revelation 15:1)

Paul accused people and he warned them saying:

> *'But in accordance with your hardness and your impenitent heart you are treasuring up for yourself wrath in the day of wrath and revelation of the righteous judgment of God.'*
> (Romans 2:5)

I said before that God vented His anger at the Cross, and He did. He judged His son there, without mercy. When Jesus cried out *'It is finished'* He was saying that God had poured out His anger and punishment of sin, completely. But, this only becomes true for those who take advantage of His salvation. If we do not do so, then the wrath of God will be poured out upon us at the Great Day.

Christians are judged in a different way from those who are not Christians. There are those who are damned because they rejected Jesus, but those who are saved, are judged according to the way they followed Jesus. The Judgement Seat of Christ is the place where Christians are judged and rewarded, and this happens on another occasion.

I refer more fully to the Judgement Day in my book *Heaven and Hell* published by Sovereign World.

Chapter 9

Man's Greatest Crime

What is this crime? Is it murder, rape, genocide, racial hatred, financial greed, abuse of human rights? Is it disobeying the laws of the land? Certainly, all these things are bad, and all these crimes merit punishment, but in the last analysis all sin is against God, not against mankind. The Bible says that all sin is against God primarily, sin against another human being is actually secondary. So what is the greatest crime mankind can commit?

It is the Crime of Rejecting Jesus, the Only Saviour

None of the sins mentioned before are as bad as the major crime committed by mankind, which is rejecting the Son of God. God warns us that He will come one day to show how deeply He feels the insult to His Son. He will come, as the Bible says:

> *'in flaming fire taking vengeance on those who do not know God, and on those who do not obey the gospel of our Lord Jesus Christ.'*   (2 Thessalonians 1:8)

This refers to those who reject Jesus.

God is so angry with those who reject Jesus that He utters this fearful warning, although the first part of the verse is wonderful.

> *'He who believes in the Son has everlasting life; and he who does not believe the Son shall not see life, but the wrath of God abides on him.'*   (John 3:36)

This is a most terrible phrase, *'The wrath of God abides on him.'* It keeps on abiding, it stays on him, or her, forever and ever.

It Involved Disobeying the Greatest Commandment

Jesus mentioned the greatest commandment:

> *'Jesus said to him, "You shall love the LORD your God with all your heart, with all your soul, and with all your mind."'*
> (Matthew 22:37)

So, we either love God with everything, or we don't love God at all.

Rejecting Jesus means that we reject the command to put Him first in our lives. In other words, to love Him more than any other, and to seek His kingdom before all else.

If the above verse is the greatest command of all, then the greatest crime is to refuse to obey it. Loving Jesus wholeheartedly, and seeking His kingdom first, is the evidence that we are born again, and that we have accepted Him as Lord. If we love Him, we obey Him.

Why is This Crime So Serious?

Refusing the great salvation from the hand of the Lord Jesus and refusing to love God with everything we have is the greatest crime, or one of the greatest crimes perhaps. But why is this so serious? Firstly, it is serious because by rejecting Jesus, we commit the crime of rejecting God's great love, which was shown to us in the life and actions of Jesus.

> *'...the Son of God, who loved me and gave Himself for me.'*
> (Galatians 2:20)

God could give no greater proof of His love than by giving His own beloved Son. If we throw this love in His face, we cannot expect anything in return, but His fierce anger.

Secondly, this crime is serious because by committing it, we reject God's costly way of escape through Jesus.

'Jesus said to him, "I am the way, the truth, and the life. No one comes to the Father except through Me."' (John 14:6)

Jesus is the only way of escape, the only way of salvation. If we reject Him, we reject everything. There is no other way of escape.

In the near future, church leaders may well be imprisoned if they preach this dogmatic statement of Jesus, that He is the way, the truth, and the life. The world will say we must be more tolerant in our preaching. We must make room for other religions, and remember that there are other ways to God also. But Jesus was not tolerant to evil, or any other doctrine, so how then can we be tolerant? Our intolerance might cause us to lay down our lives, but at least we will not have to bear the anger of God and His reproach when we stand at the Judgement Seat to give an account of what we did, and what we didn't do.

If we reject the Saviour, we are supposing that we are good enough already, and that we don't need Him. This is tremendous pride and arrogance. In fact, it is a crime against ourselves, because we will be refusing the only way of safety from Hell.

This Crime Is the Greatest Cause of God's Anger

If rejecting Jesus and failing to love God with everything that we have is the greatest crime in the world, then it must be the greatest cause of God's anger. Therefore, it merits the greatest punishment God can impose on the human race, which is consignment to Hell forever. (See my book *Heaven and Hell*, published by Sovereign World.)

Chapter 10

The Only Escape Route

One reason why I enumerated so many causes of God's anger is to arouse both Christians and non-Christians to the reality of God's emotions, particularly His anger. I do this in the hope that those who are guilty will quickly repent, find mercy, forsake their sin and walk with God in the wonderful, enjoyable, paths of righteousness.

There is only one way to escape from God's anger, whether we are Christians or non-Christians. It is through Jesus, the only Saviour and the only High Priest mediator. He alone can forgive, cleanse and renew us, so that we are fit to walk in this pathway of holiness. We must realise this, and I hope that we will fear to miss the way of escape which Jesus alone offers us.

There is a Right Fear and a Wrong Fear

In the world there is much wrong fear, because there is a lot of talk about the end of the world. People are fearful saying, 'what about the bomb, what about the population explosion, and the consequent shortage of food? How many wars are we going to see?' Many are so fearful that they are breaking down, just as Jesus said they would.

> '...men's hearts failing them from fear and the expectation
> of those things which are coming on the earth, for the powers
> of heaven will be shaken.'   (Luke 21:26)

People say, 'Is there any escape from this fear, and these awful situations?' Naturally speaking, the answer is 'no'. But, spiritually speaking, the answer is 'yes'. The trouble is that people are asking the wrong questions because they are looking at a lesser danger. Indeed, there are dangers in this world, but they are nothing like the dangers in the next world. People are more fearful of war, suffering and famine than they are afraid of the anger of God. The fear of the dangers in the world is an unhealthy fear, although understandable. But the fear of God is a healthy fear. The one destroys us, the other can save us.

Even Christians Are Afraid

We cannot close our eyes to the horrific events all around us, and because we are still humans as Christians, we do suffer from fear. But, for a Christian to be fearful is actually a sin. Hundreds of times in the Bible we are told not to be afraid, and it gives reasons why we should not be. Here are some of them:

> *'Fear not, for I am with you;*
> *Be not dismayed, for I am your God.*
> *I will strengthen you,*
> *Yes, I will help you,*
> *I will uphold you with My righteous right hand.'*
>
> (Isaiah 41:10)

> *'. . . teaching them to observe all things that I have commanded you; and lo, I am with you always, even to the end of the age. Amen.'*   (Matthew 28:20)

> *'Let your conduct be without covetousness; be content with such things as you have. For He Himself has said, "I will never leave you nor forsake you."'*   (Hebrews 13:5)

Doubting these wonderful promises and giving way to wrong fear angers God. The wise thing to do is to confess fear as a sin, turn from it as an act of the will, i.e. repentance, receive His forgiveness, which is always wholehearted and readily given, and then make sure we retain our acceptance of it.

The Main Question for a Christian

This, for Christians, is not whether we should fear circumstances, but should we fear God and His anger? The answer is

that we **should** fear the anger of God. The Bible exhorts us to
have this healthy fear.

> *'Fear God and keep His commandments,*
> *For this is man's all.'*   (Ecclesiastes 12:13)

If we do not obey all that God commands us, then we are
either backslidden or not Christians at all. Again, we turn to
Scripture:

> *'...Fear God and give glory to Him.'* (Revelation 14:7)

If there is known sin in our lives we cannot really say that we
fear God – in fact we don't. If we harbour sin we don't fear
God.

Although Christians are children of God, we are still
subject to our Father's fatherly discipline, and it can be
severe.

> *'For whom the* Lord *loves He chastens, and scourges every*
> *son whom He receives.'*   (Hebrews 12:6)

I have mentioned before, that God even took the lives of
two of His saints because they had aroused His anger by lying
to the Holy Spirit. I have seen the same thing happen in our
day. Sadly I have seen God take away some of His people
because they lied against the Holy Spirit.

When Jesus looked at Peter just after he had denied Him
and turned traitor, what did Peter see in the eyes of God the
Son? I am sure that he saw compassion, but I suspect that he
also saw anger in those holy eyes. When we see Jesus at the
Judgement Seat of Christ, to give an account of our lives, what
will we see in those same eyes? If we live in the healthy fear of
God and His holy anger, we will see love and approval in His
eyes. If we don't live in the healthy fear of God then, although
He will still be compassionate and we will not lose our
salvation, there is the possibility of judgement at that throne,
because there will still be the anger against unrighteousness.

God's Anger Can Be Turned Away

This is true for Christians and for non-Christians. There is an
escape route. This is good news, perhaps the best news in this

book. How wonderful that there is an escape route for mankind from God's anger. But the serious news is that escape is only possible in and through Jesus Christ and what He did at the Cross. It would be so foolish to ignore the good news. Better to join the Christians, who have found safety, and who, as it says in Scripture:

> '... wait for His Son from heaven, whom He raised from the dead, even Jesus who delivers us from the wrath to come.'
>
> (1 Thessalonians 1:10)

It Can Be Turned Away by Repentance

Repentance is primarily an act of the will, but it must be genuine. Partial repentance does not assuage the anger of God at all. Professing to walk in the light, in other words, walking with God in good healthy fellowship, while flirting with darkness, is sheer hypocrisy and a dangerous pursuit. God calls such people liars:

> 'He who says, "I know Him," and does not keep His commandments, is a liar, and the truth is not in him.'
>
> (1 John 2:4)

Many Christians keep up appearances at church of walking with God and living a holy life, while at the same time nursing grudges and hatred against another member. And, again, God says about such people:

> 'He who says he is in the light, and hates his brother, is in darkness until now.'   (1 John 2:9)

How can such a hypocrite be anywhere near God? Let the anger of God be a healthy deterrent to this sinful attitude. Let the anger of God help us and persuade us to walk with integrity and holiness.

King David was convicted of his sin and he repented of it. God heard his cry and changed his mind about judgement, but only when He saw David's wholehearted repentance. This is seen in 2 Samuel 24:10–16.

The Bible records many instances of repentance and God's reaction to it. Even the cruel people of Nineveh found mercy when they turned from their sin (Jonah 3:10). When some-one in the nation of Israel sinned by hiding stolen property and pretending he didn't have it, he brought trouble on the rest of his nation. But when that nation repented of their sin, and executed the criminal, God turned from His anger (Joshua 7:26).

If God convicts you, don't try and hide your sin, go to God and own up. Be honest about it, and respond while you have the chance. Remember the scripture where God says there can be an end to His patience:

> *'He will not always strive with us,*
> *Nor will He keep His anger forever.'*   (Psalm 103:9)

In other words, God offers mercy but does not have to plead with us continually to accept it.

It Can Be Turned Away by Faith in the Son of God

Centuries ago mankind sinned so badly that God decided to express His anger by flooding the earth. Noah, the one righteous man left, was warned by God about this impending judgement, and he obeyed God's instruction to build an ark. Of course, he was laughed and jeered at, possibly rejected from fellowship with his fellow man, and treated as a madman, but he trusted the Word of God, built the ark, brought his family into it, took advantage of the way of escape and did not perish with the rest of mankind. This is seen in Hebrews 11:7.

Similarly, God has made a way of escape for our genera-tion, and we will be delivered from God's wrath only if we put our trust in Jesus.

But God's Anger Can Be Turned Back on Mankind

God's anger is permanent in Hell. His anger will remain there forever. But this does not mean that every time He looks at Hell (if He looks at Hell), He will erupt in anger. It is probably better to say that those in Hell will suffer the effects of His anger there.

The things that will make His anger permanent against those in Hell are the things that they did on the earth. Because they did not repent of them on earth, there is punishment for them forever. I have mentioned them previously, so that if we are guilty of any of these sins, we might repent of them, find forgiveness while we are still alive, and avoid the risk of God's eternal anger in Hell. It can be turned back from mankind.

The foretaste of His anger which we may experience whilst still on earth, is meant to warn us of the possibility that it can be a permanent experience in Hell, where God finally expresses it.

If sins are not confessed and forgiven, those who commit them reap the awful consequences. Sinners will be punished on the Day of Judgement when God's anger is manifested against them. But, the carrying out of the sentence will take place in Hell, where there is that unending experience of His anger that I have spoken of before, but with no opportunity to cry for His mercy.

Hell Is Necessary So That God's Anger Can Be Expressed

Hell is an unpopular doctrine today, but we are foolish indeed if we neglect it. God gave mankind a choice. An eternal Heaven, or an eternal Hell. Man must have this choice, but God must also have a choice. He has decided to bar unforgiven sinners from His home so there has to be a place for them to dwell in, apart from His presence. That place is Hell. God will never vent His anger in Heaven, there is nothing to arouse it, so there must be a place where it is vented.

God's anger is more an attitude than a mere torrent of angry words. There is an eternal experience of His silence in Hell, for God has nothing to say to the occupants. He has said it all before, through the Bible. It is a dreadful thing to experience God's silence, which is why David, the Psalmist, pleaded with God in the words of Scripture:

> *'To You I will cry, O LORD my Rock:*
> *Do not be silent to me,*
> *Lest, if You are silent to me,*
> *I become like those who go down to the pit.'*   (Psalm 28:1)

Escape God's Wrath Now While You Have the Chance

May God help us who are Christians to be more faithful in warning those people who are not, to escape from this dreadful experience of the wrath of God, while they can still do so. For those reading this book who are not Christians, let me implore you in the Name of Jesus to run to Him for mercy and salvation while you are still alive.

Jesus did not beat about the bush when He spoke to the church leaders of Israel. He asked them the question:

> *'But when He saw many of the Pharisees and Sadducees coming to His baptism, He said to them, "Brood of vipers! Who warned you to flee from the wrath to come?"'*
>
> (Matthew 3:7)

This scripture poses the question – who warned the Pharisees and Sadducees to run from the wrath to come? Perhaps it was John the Baptist who did so. My point is that Jesus plainly spoke about a great day to come in which God would pour out His anger. We need to be ready to avoid it by copying the jailer in Philippi who cried out after the earthquake had smashed up his prison, and he was afraid of being executed for failing in his duty.

He cried out the words:

> *'Sirs, what must I do to be saved?'*   (Acts 16:30)

The answer is a very simple one, but it is not an easy answer because of the cost of following Jesus.

> *'So they said, "Believe on the Lord Jesus Christ, and you will be saved, you and your household."'*   (Acts 16:31)

It is not easy to be a Christian, but it is simple. The Christian life is a life of obedience to everything that God says to us by way of commandment. Those who obey are blessed, those who disobey are judged. Let us remember in closing this chapter that decisions we make in this life decide where we will be in the next life.

Chapter 11

Finally

A Note to the Unsaved

At the Judgement Throne of God in the last day, I believe that God may only ask one question, I have mentioned this before, and I repeat it again for emphasis. The question will be to the unsaved, 'What did you do with My Son Jesus? Did you surrender your life to Him, or not?' Of course, God, who is all knowing, knows the answer already. But He will require everyone to answer in the hearing of all the inhabitants of Heaven, and all who have ever lived, and the hosts of angels there. No one will be allowed to remain silent on that occasion.

Surely it is better to decide now what the answer will be, and the best answer to give on that great day is, 'Yes, Lord, I received Your Son, I surrendered to Him.'

Remember that there are three things that never return. The speared arrow, the spoken word and a lost opportunity. God grant that the opportunities that we have today, while we are alive, will not be missed.

The alternatives offered to sinners are the eternal love of a loving father, or the eternal anger of a righteous judge. If you are reading this book you are obviously alive, therefore, you have the chance to choose. Please hear the words of Scripture where God sets before us a choice.

> 'I call heaven and earth as witnesses today against you, that
> I have set before you life and death, blessing and cursing;
> therefore choose life, that both you and your descendants
> may live.'   (Deuteronomy 30:19)

A Note to the Saved

To those who are Christians I say, be prepared for the Judgement Seat of Christ, where all our words, deeds and thoughts will be made bare in the sight and hearing of all in Heaven. Check the following references and see what I mean: Hebrews 4:30; Romans 14:12; Matthew 12:36; Jude 1:15; Psalm 94:11.

One final thing to rejoice about. Mercifully, the sins that have been confessed and forgiven, and cleansed, will not be read out. Praise God for that.

Appendix

Praying for the Nation and Its Leaders

If we believe that God is angry with our nation, and that He is judging it, what shall we do about it? Shrug our shoulders and hope for the best? Or leave it to those who specialise in intercession? Surely if we believe the Bible we should get down to earnest prayer for the land:

> *'If My people who are called by My name will humble themselves, and pray and seek My face, and turn from their wicked ways, then I will hear from heaven, and will forgive their sin and heal their land.'* (2 Chronicles 7:14)

This verse is much quoted today, but I am not sure that the Church responds to it sufficiently.

God is judging all nations. They all belong to Him. Because there are so many of them brushing aside His laws He is responding in judgement. The UK is such a nation, and its safety depends largely on the prayers of the intercessors. I have been one of them for many years and I submit the following to help all those who pray, or who lead prayer meetings.

> *'I urge, then, first of all, that requests, prayers, intercession and thanksgiving be made for everyone – for kings and all those in authority, that we may live peaceful and quiet lives in all godliness and holiness. This is good, and pleases God our Savior, who wants all men to be saved and to come to a knowledge of the truth.'* (1 Timothy 2:1–4)

Include the following key aspects of national life and government:

- the judicial system
- the police force
- the financial system
- business
- church leaders
- the educational system.

There several ways to change the nation
Witnessing

> 'But when they did not find them, they dragged Jason and some other brothers before the city officials, shouting: "These men who have caused trouble all over the world have now come here."'   (Acts 17:6)

Holy living

> 'You are the salt of the earth. But if the salt loses its saltiness, how can it be made salty again? It is no longer good for anything, except to be thrown out and trampled by men.'   (Matthew 5:13)

Good works

> 'In the same way, let your light shine before men, that they may see your good deeds and praise your Father in heaven.'
> (Matthew 5:16)

In prayer we re-iterate God's promises – and believe them

> 'For no matter how many promises God has made, they are "Yes" in Christ. And so through Him the "Amen" is spoken by us to the glory of God.'   (2 Corinthians 1:20)

Let's use one of the best known prayer promises, but remember God's IF . . .

> 'If My people, who are called by My name, will humble themselves and pray and seek My face and turn from their wicked ways, then will I hear from heaven and will forgive their sin and will heal their land.'   (2 Chronicles 7:14)

IF we humble ourselves

> *'Humble yourselves in the sight of the Lord, and He will lift you up.'*   (James 4:10)

> *'Therefore humble yourselves under the mighty hand of God, that He may exalt you in due time.'*   (1 Peter 5:6)

> *'For it is time for judgement to begin with the family of God; and if it begins with us, what will the outcome be for those who do not obey the gospel of God?'*   (1 Peter 4:17)

IF we pray

> *'Then Jesus told His disciples a parable to show them that they should always pray and not give up.'*   (Luke 18:1)

> *'I want men everywhere to lift up holy hands in prayer, without anger or disputing.'*   (1 Timothy 2:8)

IF we seek God's face

> *'When You said, "Seek My face,"*
> *My heart said to You, "Your face, LORD, I will seek."'*
>   (Psalm 27:8)

We cleanse ourselves, and pray till we can 'see His face'.

IF we turn from evil

> *'Say to them: "As I live," says the Lord GOD, "I have no pleasure in the death of the wicked, but that the wicked turn from his way and live. Turn, turn from your **evil ways**! For why should you die, O house of Israel?"'*   (Ezekiel 33:11)

Sometimes we need to mourn before God

Mourning is different from being merely miserable.

We can learn so much from Bible-people who feared God's anger and who prayed that it might be averted.

Consider these serious scriptures:

> *'For the leaders of this people cause them to err,*
> *And those who are led by them are destroyed.'*
>   (Isaiah 9:16)

'The princes of Judah [**leaders**] *are like those who remove a landmark;*
I will pour out my wrath on them like water.' (Hosea 5:10)

'Her **priests** *have violated My law and profaned My holy things; they have not distinguished between the holy and unholy, nor have they made known the difference between the unclean and the clean; and they have hidden their eyes from My Sabbaths, so that I am profaned among them. Her* **princes** *in her midst are like wolves tearing the prey, to shed blood, to destroy people, and to get dishonest gain Her* [false] **prophets** *plastered them with untempered mortar, seeing false visions, and divining lies for them, saying, "Thus says the Lord God," when the Lord had not spoken. The people of the land have used oppressions, committed robbery, and mistreated the poor and needy; and they wrongfully oppress the stranger.'* (Ezekiel 22:26–29)

We need to confess our national sin

I do not believe that we can repent for the nation, because repentance is an act of the will. We are not the nation's will! But we can express our sorrow for it, and we can apologise for it.

Daniel mourned, and confessed Israel's sin

Daniel said:

'Then I set my face toward the Lord God to make request by prayer and supplications, with fasting, sackcloth, and ashes. And I prayed to the Lord my God, and made confession, and said, "O Lord, great and awesome God, who keeps His covenant and mercy with those who love Him, and with those who keep His commandments, we have sinned and committed iniquity, we have done wickedly and rebelled, even by departing from Your precepts and Your judgments. Neither have we heeded Your servants the prophets, who spoke in Your name to our kings and our princes, to our fathers and all the people of the land.

"O Lord, righteousness belongs to You, but to us shame of face, as it is this day; to the men of Judah, to the inhabitants of Jerusalem and all Israel, those near and those far off in all

the countries to which You have driven them, because of the unfaithfulness which they have committed against You. O Lord, to us belongs shame of face, to our kings, our princes, and our fathers, because we have sinned against You. To the Lord our God belong mercy and forgiveness, though we have rebelled against Him.

"We have not obeyed the voice of the LORD our God, to walk in His laws, which He set before us by His servants the prophets. Yes, all Israel has transgressed Your law, and has departed so as not to obey Your voice; therefore the curse and the oath written in the Law of Moses the servant of God have been poured out on us, because we have sinned against Him. And He has confirmed His words, which He spoke against us and against our judges who judged us, by bringing upon us a great disaster; for under the whole heaven such has never been done as what has been done to Jerusalem. As it is written in the Law of Moses, all this disaster has come upon us; yet we have not made our prayer before the LORD our God, that we might turn from our iniquities and understand Your truth. Therefore the LORD has kept the disaster in mind, and brought it upon us; for the LORD our God is righteous in all the works which He does, though we have not obeyed His voice.

"And now, O Lord our God, who brought Your people out of the land of Egypt with a mighty hand, and made Yourself a name, as it is this day; we have sinned, we have done wickedly! O Lord, according to all Your righteousness, I pray, let Your anger and Your fury be turned away from Your city Jerusalem, Your holy mountain; because for our sins, and for the iniquities of our fathers, Jerusalem and Your people are a reproach to all those around us.

"Now therefore, our God, hear the prayer of your servant, and his supplications, and for the Lord's sake cause Your face to shine on Your sanctuary, which is desolate. O my God, incline Your ear and hear; open Your eyes and see our desolations, and the city which is called by Your name; for we do not present our supplications before You because of our righteous deeds, but because of Your great mercies. O Lord, hear! O Lord, forgive! O Lord, listen and act! Do not delay for

*Your own sake, my God, for Your city and Your people are
called by Your name."*

*Now while I was speaking, praying, and confessing my sin
and the sin of my people Israel, and presenting my supplica-
tion before the* Lord *my God for the holy mountain of my
God.'* (Daniel 9:3–20)

As we mourn we can cry out for mercy

*'Do not abhor us, for Your name's sake;
Do not disgrace the throne of Your glory.
Remember, do not break Your covenant with us.
Are there any among the idols of the nations that can cause
    rain?
Or can the heavens give showers?
Are You not He, O* Lord *our God?
Therefore we will wait for You,
Since You have made all these.'* (Jeremiah 14:21–22)

'O Lord, *I have heard your speech and was afraid;
O* Lord, *revive Your work in the midst of the years!
In the midst of the years make it known;
In wrath* **remember mercy.**' (Habakkuk 3:2)

So then:

Take courage – God does relent ...

' "You have forsaken Me," says the Lord,
*"You have gone backward.
Therefore I will stretch out My hand against you and
    destroy you;
I am weary of relenting!" '* (Jeremiah 15:6)

*'If that nation against whom I have spoken turns from its
evil, I will relent of the disaster that I thought to bring upon
it.'* (Jeremiah 18:8)

'Nevertheless He regarded their affliction,
When He heard their cry; ...
And relented according to the multitude of His mercies.'
(Psalm 106:44–45)

... if we stand in the gap

> 'So I sought for a man among them who would make a wall, and stand in the gap before Me on behalf of the land, that I should not destroy it; but I found no one.'   (Ezekiel 22:30)

Will you stand in the gap, and possibly avert God's anger from our nation?